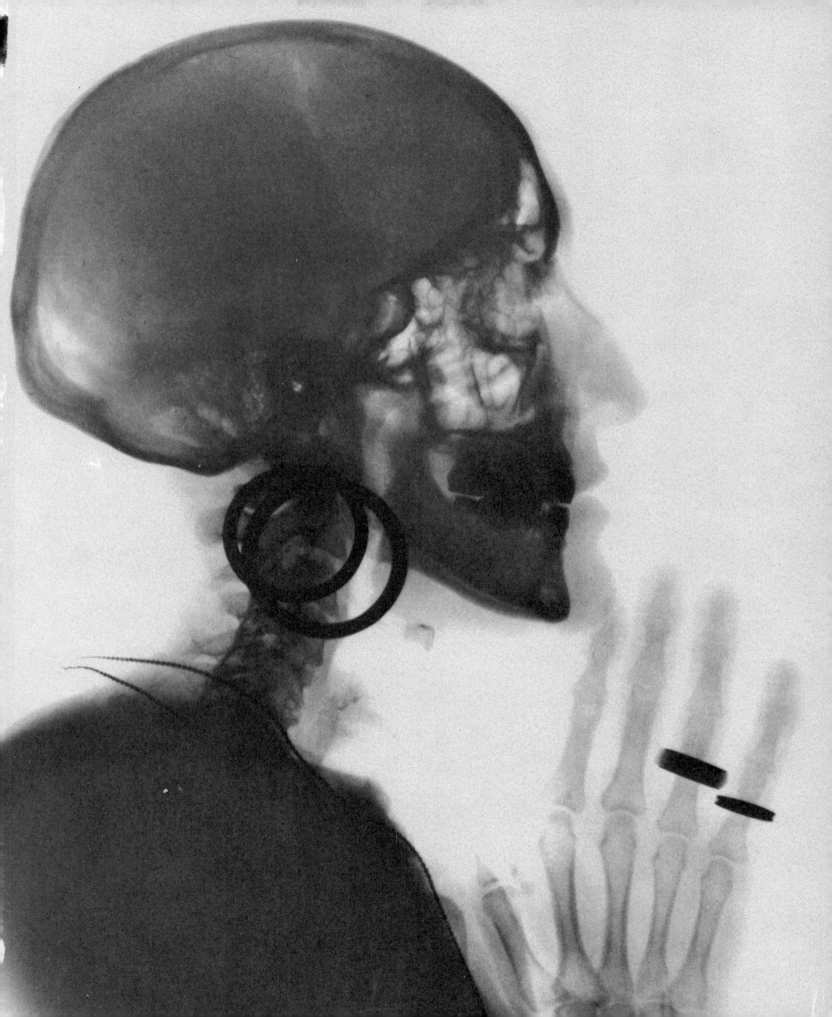

Meret Oppenheim

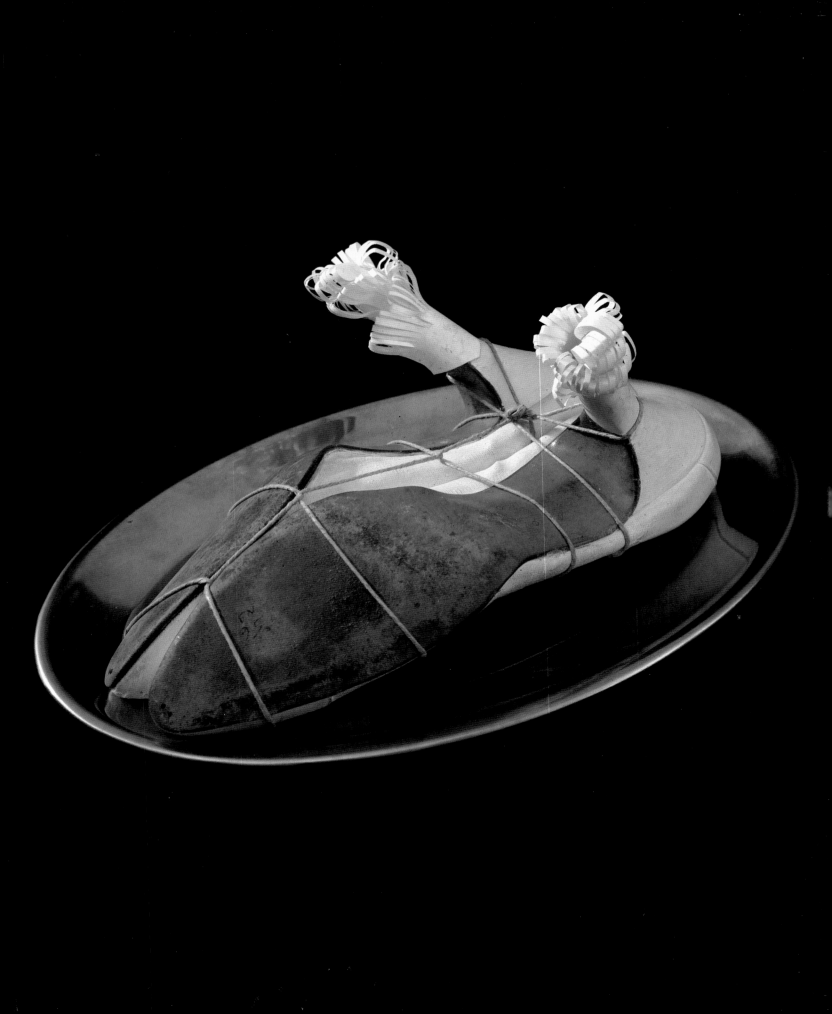

Meret Oppenheim

BEYOND THE TEACUP

JACQUELINE BURCKHARDT AND BICE CURIGER

JOSEF HELFENSTEIN

THOMAS MCEVILLEY

NANCY SPECTOR

Independent Curators Incorporated, New York
and D.A.P./Distributed Art Publishers, New York

Published in conjunction with the traveling exhibition, *Meret Oppenheim: Beyond the Teacup*, organized and circulated by Independent Curators Incorporated (ICI), New York. Guest curators for the exhibition: Jacqueline Burckhardt and Bice Curiger.

Exhibition Itinerary

Guggenheim Museum
New York, New York
June 28–October 9, 1996

Museum of Contemporary Art
Chicago, Illinois
November 2, 1996–January 11, 1997

Bass Museum of Art
Miami Beach, Florida
February 6–April 6, 1997

Joslyn Art Museum
Omaha, Nebraska
May 10–July 6, 1997

© 1996 Independent Curators Incorporated
799 Broadway, Suite 205, New York, NY 10003
Tel: 212-254-8200   Fax: 212-477-4781
e-mail: ici@inch.com

Senior Project Director: Judith Olch Richards
Editor: Robbie Capp
Designer: Russell Hassell
Printer: The Studley Press
Bindery: Horowitz / Rae

Translation Credits:

Dr. Christoph Eggenberger's foreword translated from the German by Globe Language Services, Inc.

Jacqueline Burckhardt and Bice Curiger's introduction, essay, and biography translated from the German by Catherine Schelbert.

Josef Helfenstein's essay translated from the German by David Britt.

All poetry by Meret Oppenheim translated from the German by Pamela Robertson-Pearce and Anselm Spoerri.

First hardcover edition published by
D.A.P. / Distributed Art Publishers
636 Broadway, 12th floor, NY, NY 10012
Tel: 212-472-5119   Fax: 212-673-2887

Library of Congress Catalogue
Card Number: 95-081295

ISBN: 0-916365-45-x (hardcover)
0-916365-46-8 (softcover)

Photography Credits:

Roland Aellig, pages 16, 18, 19, 39, 46, plates 27, 31, 55, 61, 63, 69, 71, 100, endleaves; Ben Blackwell, plate 51: Kurt Blum, page 50, plate 49; Marc Fiennes, plate 34; Gerhard Howald, page 20, plates 24, 45; Jacqueline Hyde, plate 6; Peter Lauri, plates 41–42, 50, 53, 56, 58, 60, 64, 75, 79, 81, 93; Jean-Pierre Leloir, plate 44; Levy, plate 89; Hugo Maertens, plate 32; Oeffentliche Kunstsammlung Basel, Martin Bühler, plate 10; R. Paltrinieri, Cadro-Ti, page 6, plates 4–5, 7–9, 25, 30, 76, 77, 84, 91–92, 95, 99; George Rehsteiner, plate 3; Mario and Beatrix Schenker, plate 52; D. Widmer, plates 28, 59; Peter Willi, plates 40, 80; Albert Winkler, page 19, plates 35.

Cover: *Fur Gloves with Wooden Fingers*, 1936. Plate 17
Frontispiece: *Ma gouvernante-My Nurse-mein Kindermädchen*, 1936. Plate 16
Front endleaf: *Röntgenaufnahme des Schädels M.O. / X-Ray of M.O.'s Skull*, 1964. See page 39.
Back endleaf: Negative of *Röntgenaufnahme des Schädels M.O. / X-Ray of M.O.'s Skull*, 1964.

This exhibition and book were made possible,

in part, through generous grants from

Pro Helvetia, Arts Council of Switzerland

Fondation Nestlé pour l'Art

The National Endowment for the Arts

The Ida and William Rosenthal Foundation, Inc.

Ivy Laboratories, Inc.

The Foundation To-Life, Inc.

Additional support was provided by

Ricola Ltd.

Sandoz Foundation

Swiss Center Foundation

ICI International Associates

Anonymous

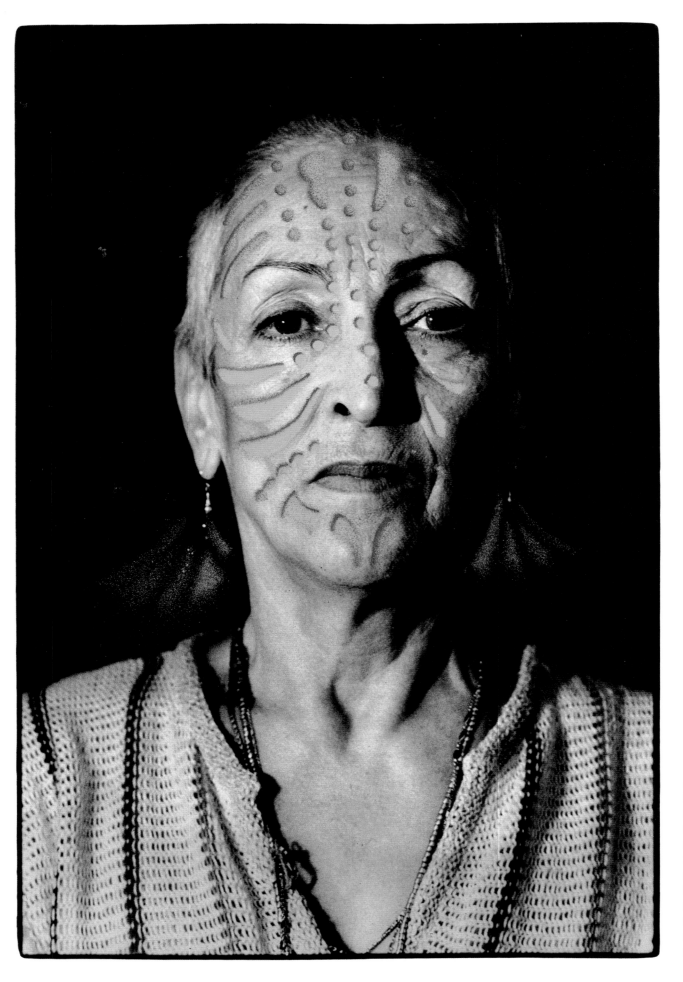

Porträt (Photo) mit Tätowierung/Portrait (Photo) with Tattoo, 1980. Stencil and spray on photograph, 11⅝ × 8¼ in (29.5 × 21 cm). Photo: Heinz Günter Mebusch, Düsseldorf, 1978. Collection Meret Schulthess-Bühler, Switzerland

Contents

In 1936 when Meret Oppenheim made the "fur teacup" she created an icon of twentieth-century art. Moreover, the fame of this object as well as the notoriety of Man Ray's photographs of her from the 1930s and those shortly before her death by other photographers such as Basel-based Christian Vogt caused her to become an icon herself. Indeed, Oppenheim's face and body became the field for works of art in themselves as evidenced by her self-portrait of 1980, *Portait (Photo) with Tattoo.*

Pro Helvetia, the Arts Council of Switzerland, has been linked to the work of Meret Oppenheim for many years, beginning with support of her notable 1981 solo exhibition, a breakthrough in the presentation of contemporary Swiss art in Austria. Using Oppenheim's *Portrait (Photo) with Tattoo* on its poster and catalogue, the exhibition traveled to museums in Vienna, Innsbruck, Klagenfurt, and Salzburg. Pro Helvetia also supported various exhibitions in Latin America that included Oppenheim's graphic work, as well as the publication of *Meret Oppenheim: Defiance in the Face of Freedom.* We are now very pleased to assist ICI with this major retrospective exhibition and the book, *Meret Oppenheim: Beyond the Teacup.*

The Swiss treasure Meret Oppenheim and her art precisely because neither she, nor it, can be classified or codified as simply Swiss. She is a Parisian from Basel with a rebellious glint in her eyes and in her work that reminds me of Carnival in Basel. Fortunately, her work evades labeling.

Even as late as 1984, shortly before her death, Meret Oppenheim was embroiled in an art scandal—all too rare in Switzerland—caused by the uproar over a fountain in Bern she designed, now much beloved by all. More than seventy years old, she could still provoke!

Dr. Christoph Eggenberger, Pro Helvetia, Arts Council of Switzerland

Meret Oppenheim in the early 1980s (Photo: Nanda Lanfranco)

Acknowledgments

The evolution of *Meret Oppenheim: Beyond the Teacup*, as both book and exhibition began in 1985 when Meret Oppenheim contributed a modest work to ICI's tenth-anniversary exhibition and silent auction. Then, during 1986 when I traveled frequently to Europe to supervise the international tour of an ICI project, I occasionally saw individual works by Oppenheim in museums or galleries, or happened to read catalogues of exhibitions that included her work. In the late 1980s, without consulting each other, two ICI guest curators, Joel Fisher and Donna Stein, selected works by Oppenheim for inclusion in their respective ICI exhibitions, *The Success of Failure* and *Contemporary Illustrated Books: Word and Image, 1967–1988*. Finally, in 1991, I arrived in Paris to find a provocative show of Meret Oppenheim's work on view at the Centre Culturel Suisse. Bit by bit, my knowledge of her work grew.

Oppenheim's earlier generosity to ICI continued to pique my curiosity about her work, as did the question of how and why she and her work could be at once so famous and so little known, especially in the United States where her fur-lined teacup, *Le déjeuner en fourrure* (1936) has been part of The Museum of Modern Art's collection since 1936. An icon of twentieth-century art, that work is as well known to artists, art historians, and students, as to the general public. Yet, to many, the artist and her gender remain unknown despite the existence of the extraordinary series of Man Ray photographs of Oppenheim in the nude. My growing knowledge of Oppenheim's work led me to view it as a precursor of the work of many younger artists, and also to believe that an American retrospective exhibition and book were imperative to redress the disparities between the infamous, famous, yet unknown Meret Oppenheim.

The final piece of my puzzle proved to be the 1989 publication in English of *Meret Oppenheim: Defiance in the Face of Freedom* by Bice Curiger. Not only had she and ICI co-curator Jacqueline Burckhardt been friends of Meret Oppenheim, but their deep knowledge of her work, her life, and her writings made them the ideal and inevitable curators of ICI's exhibition, *Meret Oppenheim: Beyond the Teacup*, and essential introductory essayists for this book.

I am grateful to Jacqueline Burckhardt and Bice Curiger for serving as ICI's guest curators, and for their generous advice and assistance, well beyond the scope of normal curatorial duties, regarding many facets of this project. Over the course of several years of preparation, this complex endeavor has involved the contributions of many people to whom I am indebted: foremost among them are Dr. Burkhard Wenger, Meret Oppenheim's brother, and other members of her family, as well as Dominique Bürgi, author with Meret Oppenheim of the catalogue raisonné contained in *Meret Oppenheim: Defiance in the Face of Freedom*, who is responsible for the Meret Oppenheim archive.

The lenders to the exhibition on page 174 have been extremely generous. I thank each of them for parting with these very special works of art for an extended period of time. Josef Helfenstein, Thomas McEvilley, and Nancy Spector have added considerably to the body of knowledge about Meret Oppenheim and her work; their insights and scholarship are invaluable. On behalf of Jacqueline Burckhardt and Bice Curiger, I would like to thank Severino Crivelli, Pio Fontana, Parkett-Verlag Zurich, and Catherine Schelbert. For ICI's staff, I acknowledge the invaluable assistance of Céline Bürgi, Nathalie Leleu, Thomas Levy, Curt Marcus, Nelly Munthe, Pamela Robertson-Pearce, Douglas Walla, and Renée Ziegler.

Lukas Gloor, Consul General of Switzerland in New York, whose tremendous enthusiasm for this exhibition and book buoyed our spirits from the moment of our first meetings, provided essential introductions to the exhibition's major funders, Pro Helvetia, the Arts Council of Switzerland, and the Foundation Nestlé pour l'Art. Important funding was also obtained from the National Endowment for the Arts, The Ida and William Rosenthal Foundation, Inc., Ivy Laboratories, Inc., and The Foundation To-Life, Inc. Additional support was provided by Ricola Ltd., the Sandoz Foundation, the Swiss Center Foundation, the ICI International Associates, and an anonymous donor. On behalf of ICI's Board of Trustees and staff, I sincerely thank all of these generous funders; their underwriting is intrinsic to the project's success.

I am keenly aware of the combined efforts of ICI's dedicated staff—Judith Olch Richards, Virginia Strull, Lyn Freeman, Jack Coyle, Alyssa Sachar, Heather Glenn Junker, Stephanie Spalding, Céline Fribourg, and Linda Obser—each of whom played a special role in bringing both exhibition and book into existence. In particular, I would like to thank Lyn Freeman, Alyssa Sachar, and Céline Fribourg for their devotion to this international project, and for their determination and perseverance in obtaining important loans and photographs. Judith Olch Richards has served as an extremely able Senior Project Director: she deserves my very special thanks. Editor Robbie Capp graciously attended to the myriad details of this publication and, as always, Russell Hassell's outstanding work as designer makes this book especially handsome.

As this exhibition opens in June 1996, it celebrates not only Meret Oppenheim and her work but also ICI's twenty-first anniversary. Throughout these years, ICI's Board of Trustees has been loyal, steadfast, extremely generous and unfailingly supportive of ICI's adventurous exhibitions. Once again, I am delighted to thank the Trustees, one and all, for their devotion to ICI's mission.

Susan Sollins, Executive Director Emerita

Introduction

Much can be learned from the remarkable oeuvre of German-born Swiss artist Meret Oppenheim (1913–1985). Her reputation was firmly established with *Le déjeuner en fourrure*, the famous fur-covered cup, saucer, and spoon, made when she was twenty-three. When Alfred Barr Jr. bought the work for The Museum of Modern Art, New York, in 1936, Meret Oppenheim was in the limelight of the international Surrealist avant-garde in Paris. Personal concerns and the turmoil of the war led her to return to Switzerland in the late 1930s, where she lived for many years in the shadow of a private life. A few decades before her death, she again became the focus of public attention.

The common and exclusive classification of Oppenheim as a Surrealist, imposed upon her since the 1930s, is only a very partial truth. The weakness of such classification becomes instantly apparent on exploring the principles that were Oppenheim's lifelong guide: the unity of her life and work, which went hand in hand with an uncompromising view of both social and artistic conventions. The aesthetic that follows from these principles and the long-standing concerns that motivated her are the subject of our opening essay, "An Enormously Tiny Bit of a Lot."

Josef Helfenstein's "Against the Intolerability of Fame" further analyzes Oppenheim's classification as a Surrealist and examines the questionable impact the renowned "fur cup" had on the artist's entire career. Oppenheim's position in the artistic and literary circles of Paris in the 1930s as artist, muse, and especially as a model and partner on equal terms with Man Ray provides the point of departure for Nancy Spector's penetrating analysis, "Performing Identities."

The artist's questioning of identity, another lifelong preoccupation, targets the fragility caused by realizing that we are not the center of the universe. Her search also reveals the richness of a world that embraces many realities. In his essay "Basic Dichotomies in Meret Oppenheim's Work," Thomas McEvilley elucidates this search and shows that the opposition between nature and culture goes back to the earliest "Surrealist" pieces.

Meret Oppenheim has left a legacy whose specific weight radiates a challenging freshness, especially from the vantage point of the outgoing twentieth century. She expressed her concerns—gender, nature/culture, the cosmos, the reality of dreams—both in visual art and in writing with a broad palette of emotions from profound alienation to witty eroticism. Such artistic and emotional diversity is but one explanation for her continuing appeal to younger generations of artists.

Jacqueline Burckhardt and Bice Curiger

Meret Oppenheim in a paper jacket she created for an Italian designer, 1976 (Photo: Claude Lê Anh)

An Enormously Tiny Bit of a Lot

Jacqueline Burckhardt and Bice Curiger

The mythical significance of the "fur teacup," *Le déjeuner en fourrure / Breakfaft in Fur*, 1936 (plate 15), does not necessarily cast its specific light on the woman who created it but rather on the history of art in the twentieth century, in the course of which a perfectly casual, lighthearted creation has been transformed into a fetish of historic impact. The work and its creator have been stored away on the shelves of art like Siamese twins preserved in formaldehyde—here the erotic, Surrealist protoproject, there the beautiful, enraptured muse—and treated as historical givens, incapable of mutual communication.

Since the late sixties, however, Meret Oppenheim has enjoyed renewed attention, apart from her dramatic "fur teacup" beginnings, particularly in Europe. The reception of her work still has currency today, although, or probably because, it could never be subsumed into any style or movement. It became clear at the time that she did not simply symbolize an era; she was, in fact, fifteen to twenty years younger than her friends of the "first hour"—the Surrealists.[1] It was felt that her individual works merited free and unfettered appreciation, in precisely the same way that she herself set out to create drawings, paintings, objects, and poetry without reliance on the routine or the security of any single style. Meret Oppenheim championed freedom with an ethical stand, for she refused to take the easy way out: "Nobody will give you freedom, you have to take it,"[2] she said.

Insatiable Curiosity

The reception of Oppenheim's work during the last two decades of her life was marked by her presence, her participation in current events, her active, fascinating response to and interest in others, and her insatiable

Meret Oppenheim at the Galerie Daniel Cordier on the occasion of the *Exposition InteRnatiOnale du Surréalisme*, 1959 (Photo: Martha Rocher)

curiosity about the doings of the younger generation. Subtle strands unite her life and her art. Certain themes were a lifelong preoccupation, literally surfacing over and over again. Closer study reveals an underlying affinity among her works that belies the superficial disjunction of her artistic production.

Over longer periods, specific motifs underwent a metamorphosis or, conversely, acquired a different content. *The Green Spectator*, an outdoor sculpture created for the Duisburg Museum in 1978, goes back to a wooden sculpture of 1959 (fig. 1, plate 41), which in turn is based on three drawings of 1933, one of which bears the title *One Person Watching Another Dying* (fig. 2). About this drawing Oppenheim commented: "The green spectator is nature indifferently watching death and life."[3]

External Appearances

Hands are also a recurring theme. In 1936, the artist designed a template for drawing the bones of a hand in white on a black leather glove. In 1942–45, she elaborated on the idea, this time drawing the engorged veins of the hand.[4] External appearances and their hidden potential have often inspired playfully serious investigations, as in the 1964 *X-Ray of M.O.'s Skull* (see p. 39), in which her chin rests on her ringed hand. This macabre self-portrait is stripped of the ephemeral facial features of Man Ray's legendary model, while the jewelry remains patently visible. Given the malicious insistence with which Oppenheim associated the "fur teacup" idea with a bracelet she designed for Elsa Schiaparelli and the fact that the gloves were fashion designs, her *X-Ray* may be read as an ironic conversion of fashionable glitz into that which endures and survives. In 1959, she made the monotypes *Five Imprints of My Hand* (fig. 3), which have been hailed as signaling a new self-awareness following years of depression.[5] These imprints in turn evoke memories of Man Ray's nude model Oppenheim standing behind the printer's wheel, her hand and arm smeared with ink up to her elbow.

Feet, or rather shoes, play an equally important role in the orchestration of Oppenheim's oeuvre. They make their first appearance in a drawing of 1934, *Why I Love My Shoes* (fig. 4), and move on in 1936 (the same year the "fur teacup" was made) to *Project for Sandals*, fur-covered high heels, and Meret Oppenheim's second-most-famous object, *Ma gouvernante—My Nurse—mein Kindermädchen* (plate 16), a pair of frilled white high heels. Tied together and served up on a silver platter, the shoes present the culinary, erotic image of a single being or a fatally intertwined unisexual couple with firm, solid thighs ready for consumption at a formal repast.[6] The object *The Couple* (see page 51, also pictured with laces tied, plate 34) of 1956 also addresses the issue of forced union, this time in a state of abandon, with shoelaces untied like a corset that has just been undone.[7]

As if to reflect the groping exploration of the creative process, the content of Oppenheim's art found its form in a broad spectrum of worlds, penetrating and expanding several realities. Her method involved letting herself drift, wide open, in a state of alert, expectant concentration.

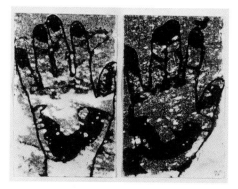

Fig. 3 Detail, *Fünf Abdrucke meiner Hand/Five Imprints of My Hand*, 1959. Monotypes, 8 ¼ × 5 ⅜ in each (21 × 13.5 cm each). Birgit and Burkhard Wenger, Basel

Focus on Nature

The artist's subject matter addresses the great issues of existence, nature, the cosmos. But the gravity of these concerns is set off against an aesthetic stand that is light, sparing, almost brittle and matter-of-fact,[8] involving—as she puts it in one of her poems—"an enormously tiny bit of a lot."[9]

The sixties saw a growing preoccupation with fog, clouds, the skies, or *Blades of Grass in the Wind* (not illustrated), as she titled a work of 1964.

And while the Surrealists turn the most ephemeral thing imaginable— passing clouds—into the solid and determined shape of a concrete wish, Meret Oppenheim's clouds remain clouds even when they are cast in bronze and stand on a bridge. They are clouds in an absolute sense, not clouds that take on one shape or another depending on the eye of the beholder, but clouds that have sprung from a multitude of potential meanings that do not cease to reverberate in them.[10]

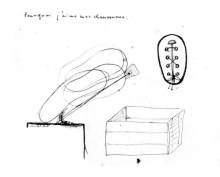

Fig. 4 *Pourquoi j'aime mes chaussures/Why I Love My Shoes*, 1934. India ink, 8¼ × 10⅝ in (21 × 27 cm). Kunstmuseum Solothurn, Switzerland

The artist's use of lines and hatching explores the borderline between volume and surface, dreaming and waking, illusion and reality, between day and night, moment and eternity. Pictures of great fragility and a precarious harmony are the result. Oppenheim's aesthetic takes a clear stand against dynamic statements and sweeping assertions.

What seems at times to be an experimental dissolution of the ego in utopian reorientation is mirrored not only in the searching, coolly beseeching line but also in rapidly drawn or painted and collaged pieces

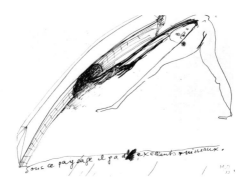

Fig. 5 *Sous ce paysage il y a d'excellents ruisseaux/ There Are Excellent Streams Beneath This Landscape*, 1933. India ink, 6⅜ × 8¼ in (16 × 21 cm). Private collection, Zurich

that explode the limits of earthly existence, as in the drawing *There Are Excellent Streams Beneath This Landscape*, 1933 (fig. 5), the collage *Paradise Is Under the Ground*, 1940 (plate 22), or in the painting *A Pleasant Moment on a Planet*, 1981 (plate 96). The exposure, the vulnerability of the artistic gesture is enhanced by the small format of most of the works and the nonhierarchical use of media and materials.

Dreams and Myth

Indifferent to artistic convention and personal fulfillment, Meret Oppenheim saw the artist as an instrument of something universal, and artistic inspiration as supraindividual.[11] This is underscored by an unwonted concept of beauty with an intentionally moral thrust: "I am aesthetically obligated to show the world beauty not out of vanity and not because I want to be beautiful, but because the world needs beauty—even when the world is no longer aware of its profound longing for beauty."[12]

The works seem to have sprung from the reality of an inner life that embraces all the senses, the conscious mind, all interpretation, and the study of dreams. Oppenheim's eroticism and humor are not a frivolous pose. The "realization of pleasure and the love of creatures and things"[13] flash like lightning across larger spaces and times. Hers is not the gravity that requires levity to make it bearable but rather the truth that surfaces in play. She has tested experience, covering a range that does not shy away from black humor and the macabre. Early ink drawings already show this predilection, as in *Suicides' Institute* (fig. 6) or the complex antichildbearing image, *Votive Picture (Strangling Angel)* (plate 1), both of 1931. Similar concerns underlie *Octavia*,[14] a picture-

Fig. 6 *Selbstmörder-Institut / Suicides' Institute*, 1931. India ink, 5½ × 8¹¹⁄₁₆ in (15 × 33 cm). Private collection

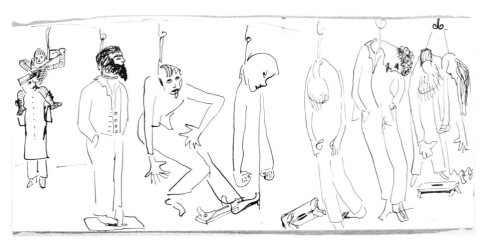

object of 1969 (plate 67). A figure with no arms is painted on a real saw, its helpless confinement standing in contrast to the gaiety of the colors, the plasticity of the image, and the lascivious play of the tongue.

The last two works above obviously deal with the role of women in society and as artists—issues that Oppenheim explored and transcended in an exemplary manner. *Genevieve* (fig. 7, plate 70), a sculpture made in 1971, also embodies the image of woman condemned to inactivity. The draft of this piece was originally made in 1942 during a period of prolonged crisis. A simple board and two broken sticks as arms evoke the legend of Genevieve of Brabant, who was unjustly accused of adultery and banned to the forest, there to live in pain and sorrow with her infant son.

Oppenheim often drew inspiration from myths but even more so from language and her own dreams. She exploits language—quite apart from its ordinary use value—as a material with unlimited potential that must be penetrated and activated. The artist's language is at its most explicit in such works as the 1934 *Quick, Quick, the Most Beautiful Vowel Is Voiding* (plate 7) and *Word wrapped in poisonous letters (Becomes transparent)* of 1970 (fig. 8). Christiane Meyer-Thoss, who has edited and published Meret Oppenheim's dreams and poems, notes that a profound longing for language marks the artist's pictures while, conversely, the poems are motivated by a determined quest for realization in the image.[15] As if language also had periods of dreaming, Oppenheim wrote in her 1980 text *Self-portrait Since 60,000 B.C. to X* (see related work, fig. 9, plate 64):

Thoughts are locked in my head as in a beehive. Later I write them down. Writing burned up when the library of Alexandria went up in flames [when Julius Caesar captured the city in 48 B.C.]. The black snake with its white head is in the museum in Paris. Then it burns down as well. All the thoughts that have ever existed roll around the earth in the huge mindsphere. The earth splits, the mindsphere bursts, its thoughts are scattered in the universe where they continue to live on other stars.[16]

Evocative Symbols

Oppenheim cuts across the space of time, culture, and nature with the speed of poetic license, and introduces, as if in play, *Old Snake Nature* (plate 68), an object of 1970 now in the Centre Georges Pompidou in

Fig. 7 *Genoveva / Genevieve*, 1971

Fig. 8 *Word wrapped in poisonous letters (Becomes transparent)*, 1970. String, hardened polyester and engraved brass plaque, mounted on a wooden board, 5½ × 12¼ × 15⅞6 in (14 × 31 × 39.5 cm) (without board). Ulmer Museum, Ulm, Germany

Fig. 9 *Selbstporträt und curriculum vitae seit dem Jahr 60,000 a.C./ Self-portrait and Curriculum Vitae Since the Year 60,000 B.C.*, 1966

Paris. A large snake made of anthracite with a white china head and green eyes lies curled up on a plain coal sack. When Oppenheim addresses the opposition of nature and culture, her choice of symbols is rich in connotation. Snakes play an exclusively positive role in her oeuvre, for instance, as an attribute of matriarchal goddesses and a symbol of the earth. She used to say that we should be grateful to the serpent for encouraging Eve to taste an apple from the tree of wisdom, for, as a result, the inhabitants of paradise became cultural beings. The serpent also symbolizes time because it sheds its skin in a process of constant renewal. The painting *The Secret of Vegetation,* 1972 (plate 73), clearly demonstrates how much this animal means in Oppenheim's oeuvre. Here, the artist's vision of essence and effect in nature comes to a climax. In a strictly vertical, deceptively symmetrical composition, two snakes wind their way upward as if in a dance of love. The two poles of energy that are their heads culminate in an extremely subtle form of opposition: The one head is blue and almond-shaped; the other, a soft-edged white sphere. Infinite agitation grips the basically static image. A vibrant whirlwind of diamond-shaped leaves and white rectangles floods the glimmering, searing light of the picture plane.[17]

A similar blend of geometric and organic shapes defines another invocation of nature entitled *Spiral (Nature's Way)* (plate 72). First made as a small sculpture in 1971, a large bronze of it cast in 1985 now stands in the fountain of the Ancienne Ecole Polytechnique in Paris. The basically symmetrical structure of this work is slightly off balance as if threatened by the contending forces of the desire for harmony and the awareness of its imminent danger. Its placement in front of the institute of technology enhances the significance of this sculpture, defining it as a monument to nature, to the forces unleashed when human beings interfere, moving into that destructive territory to which the atomic bomb belongs.

Notes

1 In numerous conversations, some of them recorded (e.g., radio broadcasts with Ruth Henry, Süddeutscher Rundfunk, September 29, 1978), Meret Oppenheim stresses that she still shares the original ideas of Surrealism, although she was never deeply involved in the movement. The misconception prevails that she was associated with the Surrealists for decades, but she actually distanced herself from them after only two years, because she could not accept the dogmatism of their political attitudes. An indispenable study on this issue is Josef Helfenstein, *Meret Oppenheim und der Surrealismus*, Stuttgart: Verlag G. Hatje, 1993.

2 Meret Oppenheim in her acceptance speech for the 1974 Art Award of the City of Basel, January 16, 1975, published in Bice Curiger, *Meret Oppenheim: Defiance in the Face of Freedom*, trans. Catherine Schelbert, Zurich: Parkett, Cambridge, Mass.: MIT Press, 1989, pp. 130–31.

3 Cf. Meret Oppenheim's comment on this work in *Meret Oppenheim*, exhibition catalogue, ARC-Musée d'Art Moderne de la Ville de Paris, 1984, p. 19.

4 The glove was produced as a special edition for the journal *Parkett*, no. 4, 1985.

5 On the subject of the hand, cf. Isabel Schulz, "*Edelfuchs und Morgenröte*" *Studien zum Werk von Meret Oppenheim*, Munich: Verlag Silke Schreiber, 1993, p. 38ff.

6 Cf. comments on this work in the interview with Meret Oppenheim: ARC catalogue, op. cit., p. 17.

7 Cf. Meret Oppenheim's comment on *The Couple* in Jean-Christophe Ammann, "For Meret Oppenheim" in Curiger, op. cit., p. 116: " . . . an odd unisexual pair: two shoes unobserved at night doing 'forbidden' things." The shoes illustrated the article "Hermaphrodite" in the EROS exhibition at the Galerie Daniel Cordier, Paris (1959–60).

8 "Every idea is born with its form. I carry out ideas the way they enter my head. Where inspiration comes from is anybody's guess but it comes with its form; it comes dressed, like Athena who sprang from the head of Zeus in helmet and breatsplate." In Curiger, op. cit., pp. 20–21. Today, many artists share this creative principle; they reserve the right to make both figurative and abstract art; they prefer nonhierarchic forms and media; they reject the grand gesture.

9 From Meret Oppenheim's poem of 1969 "Without me anyway . . ." in Curiger, op. cit., p. 112.

10 Rita Bischof, "Das Geistige in der Kunst von Meret Oppenheim," talk given at the memorial service, November 20, 1985 (private printing, n.p.).

11 See ARC catalogue, op. cit., p. 22.

12 In Bischof, op. cit. the author goes on to say, "She [M.O.] recognized beauty as genuine transcendence, a transcendence that springs from the fact that she herself shatters the intimate complexity of power and morality in the great moral entities. The morality of beauty neither judges nor condemns; it liberates."

13 Jean-Hubert Martin, in *Meret Oppenheim*, exhibition catalogue, Kunsthalle, Bern, 1982, p. 3: "There was a tendency to interpret this unbridled freedom as amateurish or dilettantish. In reality, it is nothing but the experience of a highly moral attitude that puts the realization of pleasure and the love of creatures and things above all else. The direct and immediate consequence of this is rebellion against conformity and convention."

14 Cf. Schulz, op. cit., pp. 120–21.

15 Christiane Meyer-Thoss, *Meret Oppenheim: Husch, husch, der schönste Vokal entleert sich*, poems, drawings, Frankfurt a.M., 1984, p. 119; Christiane Meyer-Thoss, ed., *Meret Oppenheim: Aufzeichnungen 1928–1985, Träume*, Bern/Berlin: Verlag Gachnang und Springer, 1986.

16 Curiger, op. cit., p. 7.

17 Cf. the detailed interpretation in Schulz, op. cit., pp. 71–74.

Against the Intolerability of Fame
Meret Oppenheim and Surrealism

Josef Helfenstein

In Europe by the mid-1970s, Meret Oppenheim had become a kind of symbolic figure. To younger generations, both in her work and in her attitude as an artist, she was a model of mental and artistic independence. As is well known, at the outset of her career Oppenheim was a member of the Surrealist movement. As a result of her dislike of the Surrealist label, questioning the nature of this relationship long remained off limits. I am convinced that despite Oppenheim's ambivalent relationship with the Surrealists, their ideas are actually fundamental to an understanding of her work. It is precisely the skewed response to her work over the past two decades—and all the reluctance to admit a Surrealist link—that has prevented any properly nuanced historical approach to Oppenheim's work.[1]

The "fur cup" (1936) played a decisive role within this context. The early fame of this object had a punishing, rather than positive, effect on Oppenheim's whole career. A glance at the contemporary historical context makes it plain that the ideological base of Surrealism contributes to our understanding of Oppenheim's work, and, conversely, that many general aims of Surrealism become more verifiable and, to some extent, open to historical criticism, by reference to the works of an artist outside the movement. For Oppenheim's work exemplifies how these objectives can be adopted, pursued, and put into practice in ways that differ importantly from the Surrealists' original intentions.

In Paris, 1932–37

Meret Oppenheim was eighteen when she traveled to Paris in May 1932 to become an artist. Through Hans Arp and Alberto Giacometti, she soon came into contact with the Surrealist circle around André Breton. At his

Meret Oppenheim in her studio
in Montrouge, 1933

suggestion, she took part in the regular meetings at the Café de la Place Blanche. Until the autumn of 1933, she lived and worked at the Hôtel Odessa in Montparnasse. Alongside her sporadic attendance at the Académie de la Grande Chaumière, she chose to work alone, at night in her hotel room or in a studio in Montrouge. Her personal encounters and friendships with several artists in or close to the Surrealist movement became a decisive point of departure for her. In her circle of friends and acquaintances, Giacometti, Arp, and Breton were soon joined by Marcel Duchamp, Man Ray, and Max Ernst. In 1934, she embarked on a passionate affair with Ernst, which lasted just under a year.[2] The fact that many outstanding intellectuals, poets, and artists were attached to the fringes of Surrealism was an important factor in the influence the movement had on young artists.

What counted for Oppenheim most of all was that Giacometti, Arp, and Ernst, all of whom were close to the Surrealists, were the first to notice and support her work. The importance of Surrealism to her was of a far more general nature than can be detected from specific stylistic choices. What influenced Oppenheim in Paris was above all acceptance and approval for the way she was living her life.

The Surrealists soon invited Oppenheim to take part in their group shows. Her first entry was at the sixth exhibition of the Surrealist-dominated "Association artistique des Surindépendants," held in Paris from October 27 to November 26, 1933.[3] She went on to contribute to major Surrealist group exhibitions in Copenhagen (1935), Paris (1935, 1936), London (1936), and New York (1936). As well as including all the established Surrealists, the big shows in London and New York exhibited work by Paul Klee, Pablo Picasso, Francis Picabia, Marcel Duchamp, and Giorgio de Chirico. These were the exhibitions at which Surrealism achieved its maximum public exposure.

In the space of barely three years, Oppenheim had thus become a regular participant in Surrealist events. Then everything changed when she became famous for *Le déjeuner en fourrure/Breakfast in Fur* (fig. 1, plate 15). In 1936, right after it had been shown first in Paris, the object was bought by Alfred H. Barr Jr. for the collection of The Museum of Modern Art in New York. Its fame grew overnight. However, the artist then began to distance herself from the Surrealists. As a result of a chronic depression suffered by Oppenheim from the mid-1930s to 1954, which she later described as a "destruction of self-esteem," she returned to Basel in 1937, where she attended the School of Arts and Crafts for two years. Following one exhibition in Amsterdam in 1938, she went back to Paris in 1939 and joined Ernst and other Surrealists in an exhibition of fantasy furniture. This was Oppenheim's last contribution to a Surrealist show for a long time. From July 1939, she lived in Switzerland and did not visit Paris again for more than ten years. It was the beginning of a long crisis.

The Impact of Breakfast in Fur

The Surrealists' response to Oppenheim's work was almost exclusively a response to her as a person, or rather to certain attributes of the person that the Surrealists liked—her beauty, youth, and rebellious attitude. These qualities were stereotyped and stylized not only by the Surrealists[5] but by art critics of the day, who barely gave mention to Oppenheim's work as an artist. This disparity between ready reception of the person and denial of her work is something that clearly befell most female artists in the Surrealist circle.[6] There are, of course, some works by Oppenheim that must have appealed to Surrealist sensibilities, since they were shown repeatedly in magazines and enthusiastically received by the public. Most were objects chosen largely because of the particular importance attached to object art by Surrealists of the 1930s—not due to any arbitrarily selective appreciation of Oppenheim's activity as an artist.

Breakfast in Fur was the work most highly valued by the Surrealists. Its title, legendarily coined by André Breton, may possibly

Fig. 2 Max Ernst, *Le déjeuner sur l'herbe*, 1936.
Oil on canvas, 18⅛ × 21⅔ in (46 × 55 cm).
Private collection

bear some associative relationship with Max Ernst's painting *Le déjeuner sur l'herbe* (fig. 2), of the same year. Both titles refer in characteristically periphrastic Surrealist language to a key work of art history, the celebrated painting by Edouard Manet. When the object was first exhibited, Oppenheim described it simply *Tasse, soucoupe et cuillère revêtus de fourrure (Cup, saucer, and spoon covered with fur)*.[7]

The first exhibition devoted to Surrealist object art took place in Paris at the Galerie Charles Ratton in May 1936 (fig. 3). It marked an early apogee of Surrealist object art, and despite its mere one-week duration, its effect as a stimulus cannot be overestimated. Organized by Breton, the occasion differed from a conventional art exhibition not only in the choice of exhibits but also in their presentation. Included were objects from nature such as crystals, carnivorous plants, plants that shrank away "modestly" when touched, a stuffed anteater, and birds' eggs, as well as objects altered by natural phenomena such as fires, storms, or volcanic eruptions. An important part of the exhibition consisted of objects from outside Europe, including cult articles, fetishes, and masks from the Americas, Africa, and Oceania. There were also a number of sculptures from Picasso's studio, never shown before, and ready-mades by Duchamp.

In addition to *Breakfast in Fur,* Oppenheim was represented by two other objects: *Head of a Drowned Person, Third State,* since lost; and the shoe object *Ma gouvernante—My Nurse—mein Kindermädchen* (figs. 4 and 5). The "fur cup" was presented on the bottom shelf of a glass case, surrounded by non-European and other objects. The same case housed sculptures by Ernst, and Duchamp's *Bottle Dryer.* Highly confusing to a visitor to the exhibition, the antiartistic presentation of numerous and varied objects in a confined space was clearly part of Breton's strategy. The juxtaposition of exotic artifacts, articles, flea-market objects, and art, the passion for the remote and the subcultural, was a direct assault on normative aesthetics. In this bewildering context, Oppenheim's fur object looked positively modest and discreet—which makes the sensation with which it was greeted all the more surprising.

Oppenheim's entry was the big hit of the exhibition—no doubt because it presented the basic principle of the Surrealist object with classic simplicity.[8] The first critic to comment on the "fur cup" was Marcel Jean, when he reviewed the exhibition for *Cahiers d'Art.* This first appreciation by a Surrealist already tended toward a sexual interpretation of the object. The same writer later attributed the work's public success to an association between food and fur: "The visitors immediately imagine themselves drinking their chocolate from this vessel."[9]

According to William S. Rubin, the object enjoyed an even greater success at the celebrated exhibition *Fantastic Art Dada Surrealism,* held at The Museum of Modern Art in New York in the winter of 1936–37. Dalí, he said, paid the Swiss artist's work the questionable compliment of adopting the idea for a fur-lined bathtub commissioned for a store window display in New York in 1939.[10] Shortly after The Museum of Modern Art exhibition closed, Barr, who had organized it jointly with the Surrealists, remarked:

Few works of art in recent years have so captured the popular imagination as has Meret Oppenheim's Surrealist object, the "fur-lined cup, plate and spoon." Like Lautréamont's renowned image, like Dalí's limp watches, the "fur-lined tea set" makes concretely real the most extreme, the most bizarre improbability. The tension and excitement caused by this object in the minds of tens of thousands of Americans have been expressed in rage, laughter, disgust or delight.[11]

The history of the early fame of *Breakfast in Fur* is one of the decisive events in Oppenheim's artistic career. When bought by Barr for the

EXPOSITION
SURRÉALISTE

D'

OBJETS

du 22 au 29 Mai 1936
de 14 h. 30 à 18 h. 30

chez

CHARLES RATTON

14, Rue de Marignan, Paris (VIIIᵉ)

Fig. 3 Announcement, *Exposition Surréaliste d'objets,* Galerie Charles Ratton, Paris, 1936

Modern shortly after it was created, the "fur cup" became part of what was soon to be the world's most preeminent collection of twentieth-century art. As a result of its spectacular success, Oppenheim's piece soon became one of the most popular of all Surrealist works. The down-side of this early fame and its associated hype, to which Man Ray's celebrated photographs made a considerable contribution, was that Oppenheim became the victim of her own work, which stuck to her like an all-distorting label. The unbalanced response was like mummification, preventing any serious engagement with her work as a whole or recognition of its fierce concern with intellectual independence. This sudden and superficial fame, coming at the very beginning of Oppenheim's career, was probably one reason for her subsequent lengthy artistic crisis.[12]

Even worse, from that moment on, whatever she did, Oppenheim was labeled a Surrealist. Not even twenty-three years old when fame hit, she was saddled with a myth of her own. For decades on end, the "fur cup" led to fundamental and persistent misapprehensions about her work. For instance, it was erroneously supposed by many that Oppenheim mainly made objects in fur.

Ever since Oppenheim was rediscovered in the 1960s–70s and her work perceived for the first time as a whole, the myth has been stood on its head. In 1982, Werner Hofmann remarked that of late, "people have imposed on themselves an ascetic duty of blocking this object out, whenever there is talk of Meret Oppenheim's art—as if she had to be shielded from her own fame."[13]

The lasting success of the "fur cup," not only with the public but also among Surrealists, must nevertheless be partly explained by the fact that with this object Oppenheim had indeed made a strong artistic statement of Surrealist theoretical ideas. This becomes evident on a close reading of Breton's essay "Crise de l'objet," published in *Cahiers d'Art* in 1936, shortly after the exhibition at the Galerie Ratton. The "fur cup," corresponding to Breton's article, realized one of his principal demands in relation to Surrealist object art: *traquer la bête folle de l'usage*—to hound the mad beast of function.[14] By this, Breton meant the subversive redefinition and mystification of the use values of objects, and ultimately, the undermining of rational conceptions. This is what Oppenheim's *Breakfast in Fur* does with striking directness.

The genesis of the piece—as retold by Oppenheim herself with tongue in cheek—is not atypical for a Surrealist work of art, and is characteristic for that reason. Since the advent of Dada, the café had been one

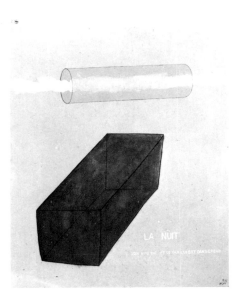

Fig. 6 *La nuit, son volume et ce qui lui est dangereux/ The Night, Its Volume and What Endangers It*, 1934

of the most important meeting places for artists, a place where opinions and ideas could be exchanged. For the Surrealists, the café represented not only social contact and a maintenance of bohemian tradition but the ideal place for "conspiracy" and for collective working. The anecdotes linked with *Breakfast in Fur*, the fortuitous meeting with Picasso in which the idea of the object arose in the course of a perfectly ordinary conversation, confirm just how characteristic the object really is of the Surrealist movement. The genesis of the object as art corresponded with rare precision to one of the principal aims of the Surrealist movement, the "collectivization of ideas" with the help of chance.

The Volume of Night

In 1934, Oppenheim painted *The Night, Its Volume and What Endangers It* (fig. 6, plate 8). For several reasons, this is a key work in her early career. It reflects her engagement with Surrealism in particularly complex ways.

Sparingly painted in ink and oil on cardboard, the image contains in its lower half a dark-blue, transparent rectangular prism above which a tubular object appears to hang in mid air. The interior of this long, yellow cylinder is penetrated by a white, gaslike, but (from its color) viscous-looking substance. White strips of color emerging from both ends make the cylinder look like a rolling-pin. The steamlike, horizontally spreading fluids cause the tubular body above to fall into mysterious contrast with the motionless, transparent block below. The elimination of detail and the object's unreal transparency add to the unfathomable quality of the picture's content. What we see is uninterpretable, persistently abstract dream imagery. Dry and chilly in both composition and execution, the image appears as a totally mysterious combination of ambiguous geometrical objects. The effect of the picture rests not least on this coolness, which is not alleviated by any trace of irony.

The spark is struck, as it were, in the vacuum between a simplistic pictorial arrangement and the enigma of its title. Written in white paint in lettering of two different sizes, the words at bottom right form part of the composition and its aesthetic effect. This scenario forces the viewer to try to find its interpretation. An enigmatic, precarious equilibrium seems to be established, which—as the title suggests—is threatened by something. Interestingly, the formulation implies a reversal of one's expectations. The threat is not associated with the night, as would normally be expected; it is the night itself that is in danger.

Fascination with the Nocturnal

The theme of this painting, night—without which the painting cannot be understood—is one with a multitude of meanings for Surrealists. As admirers of German Romanticism, the Surrealists adopted the Romantic idea of Night.[15] In their conception of "surreality," they interpreted reality as a synthesis of opposites—such as sleep and waking, life and death, the marvelous and the mundane—which they refused to accept as opposites in any dualistic sense. The fascination with night also embraced aspects of the forbidden and the abyss; it corresponded to the Surrealists' taste for black humor, crime, and the horror novel. By extension, the "unknown territory" of the night side of life automatically connected it to one of their pet themes: sexuality. For the Surrealists, night was a "place of confusion," and not only in the moral sense.

The Surrealists' attempts to mobilize the socially repressed "night side" of the human psyche and to bring out its positive power extended to the creative processes of the artist. For the Surrealists, night was filled with occult "voices of the depths," which for them were synonymous with the "source of poetry."[16] Their refusal to submit the nocturnal to the rational control of consciousness has been consistently interpreted as an alluring promise of magic.[17] The idealization of the night as the preferred "creative time" for poets and artists, as they ply their trade in isolation, is not a Surrealist invention. But in Surrealism, the night took on a significance that had no precedent except in Romanticism.

Night is a central theme of Surrealist art, and not only iconographically. Fascination with the night also reflects the movement's self image and theoretical articles of faith. It was part of the Surrealists' declared intention to make an art that would be enigmatic, obscure, and inaccessible to rational models of explanation. This negative self-definition is to some extent the starting point for any approach to their literature and art. The exaltation of night, in this context as in others, was one of the Surrealists' strategies. In a sense, as the title of Oppenheim's night painting suggests, it is to be seen in this context of deliberately intensified mystery.

The Consciousness of Detachment

Unlike Ernst's 1923 *Pietà or Revolution by Night*, or Dalí's 1937 *Sleep*, both regarded as programmatic images of Surrealism, Oppenheim's night painting has never been seen as a Surrealist work. One reason may lie in its enigmatic title, which makes it impossible to pin down the work to a coded allegory of Surrealist lifestyle—an idealization of the nocturnal. The theme's cool treatment, its frigid abstraction, and distanced conceptuality preclude the literary singleness of interpretation that is characteristic of Surrealist night paintings. Its detachment from prescribed Surrealist content may well be crucial to an understanding of this painting. *The Night, Its Volume and What Endangers It* is one of the few examples in Oppenheim's oeuvre to suggest where an intensive engagement with Surrealist iconography might have led her, and to reveal that artistically, this was quite a viable possibility.

Still more important is the painting's stylistic significance for the artist's later output. This chilly abstraction was later to become an unmistakable hallmark of her work. Its representational mode is related to the "Verismo of the Improbable" of one phase of Surrealist art. In Oppenheim's *Night* painting, this form of abstraction manifests itself as a personal style. The extreme economy of painterly means and the cool handling of colors are the preconditions of the specific form of poetry that is characteristic of Meret Oppenheim's work.

The artist has constantly emphasized the unpredetermined nature of her pictorial content, which is based on "ideas that occur," and the agreement between content and form. Even in her early work, heterogeneity and discontinuity of style show themselves as autonomous characteristics. Thus, Oppenheim's poetic method subtly but fundamentally differs from Surrealist methods based on shock effects. The allure of specific materials and the "poetry of the disparate,"[18] dominate an unequivocal statement of content. Often inspiration at the origin of the creative process seems to lie in freely playing with materials.

This artistic principle is to be found in many of Oppenheim's paintings, but above all, in her objects, from *Breakfast in Fur* onward. Often it goes together with an extreme spareness of form. In the lyrical, still, often macabre subtlety of Oppenheim's work lies one of her special qualities, and at the same time, one of the fundamental differences between her work and the provocative free association and permutation of the Surrealists. Most of Oppenheim's late work is particularly revealing in this respect. It is a manifesto against the intolerability of fame and in favor of continually renewed creativity.

Notes

1 I have made a start on this in my book *Meret Oppenheim und der Surrealismus*, Stuttgart: Verlag G. Hatje, 1993.

2 See Bice Curiger, *Meret Oppenheim: Defiance in the Face of Freedom*, trans. Catherine Schelbert, Zurich: Parkett and Cambridge, Mass.: The MIT Press, 1989, p. 18.

3 Exhibition catalogue, *Association artistique. Les surindépendants. Sixième exposition*, Paris: Parc des expositions—Porte de Versailles, October 27–November 26, 1933. The names of the Surrealists represented in the exhibition are listed at the end of the catalogue under the heading *Supplément*, without reference to the works exhibited. On Oppenheim's contribution, see her statement in *Art. Das Kunstmagazin*, June 1982, p. 24.

4 Exhibition catalogue, *Surrealistische Schilderkunst*, Amsterdam: Galerie Robert, Keizersgracht 527, 1938, without list of exhibitions. Works by Oppenheim were included in other exhibitions, including that at the Galerie des Beaux-Arts, Paris, 1938, but without any active participation on her part.

5 On the response of the Surrealists (Man Ray and Ernst in particular) to the girl they called Meretlein, see Helfenstein, op. cit., 34ff.

6 Examples are Valentine Hugo (1897–1968); Leonora Carrington (b. 1917), and Toyen (Marie Cerminova) (1902–1980). See Whitney Chadwick, *Women Artists and the Surrealist Movement*, Boston: Little, Brown, 1985, p. 10.

7 Exhibition catalogue, *Exposition Surréaliste d'objets du 22 au 29 mai 1936*, Paris: Galerie Charles Ratton, 1936. Brochure containing unnumbered work list. Breton's title *Le déjeuner en fourrure* also embodies an allusion to Leopold Sacher-Masoch's 1870 novel *Venus im Pelz (Venus in Fur)*. On this see Stuart Morgan, exhibition catalogue, *Meret Oppenheim*, London: Institute of Contemporary Arts, 1989, n.p.

8 William S. Rubin, *Surrealismus*, Stuttgart: 1979, p. 127.

9 Exhibition catalogue, *Meret Oppenheim*, Rome: Galleria La Medusa, 1969, n.p. See also Haim N. Finkelstein, *Surrealism and the Crisis of the Object*, Ann Arbor, Mich., 1979, p. 70f.

10 Rubin, op. cit., p. 127. See also Elsa Honig Fine, *Woman and Art*, Montclair and London, 1978), p. 178.

11 Alfred H. Barr Jr., "Surrealism: What It Is in Literature and the Arts, its Origin and Future," *The World Today*, vol. 4, no. 4 (April 1937), p. 4. I owe this reference to Carolyn Lanchner, who made it possible for me to examine the related file in the Department of Painting and Sculpture at The Museum of Modern Art, New York.

12 See also Josef Helfenstein, "Androgynität als Bildthema und Persönlichkeitsmodell. Zu einem Grundmotiv im Werk von Meret Oppenheim," in exhibition catalogue, *Meret Oppenheim. Legat an das Kunstmuseum Bern*, Bern: Kunstmuseum, 1987, p. 13ff. On the reception history of *Le déjeuner en fourrure*, see also Josephine Withers, "The Famous Fur-Lined Teacup and the Anonymous Meret Oppenheim," *Arts Magazine*, November 1977, p. 88ff.

13 Werner Hofmann, "Laudatio auf Meret Oppenheim," in *Kunstpreis Berlin. Grosser Kunstpreis 1982*, Berlin, 1982, p. 7f.

14 André Breton, *Cahiers d'Art*, 1936, no. 1–2, p. 22.

15 See Helfenstein, op. cit., p. 170ff.

16 Rainer Warning, "Der Traum der Surrealisten," in Lucien Dallenbach and Christiaan L. Hart Nibbrig, eds., *Fragment und Totalität*, Frankfurt am Main: Suhrkamp, 1984, p. 322.

17 "Surrealism opens the gates of the dream to all those to whom the Night shows itself niggardly. Surrealism is the crossing point of the sleep-enchanters, of alcohol, tobacco, ether, opium, cocaine, morphine . . ." Walter Benjamin, quoted by Werner Hofmann, *Grundlagen der modernen Kunst. Eine Einführung in ihre symbolische Formen*, Stuttgart: Belser, 1966, 1978, p. 406.

18 Helfenstein, op. cit., p. 88.

Meret Oppenheim
Performing Identities

Nancy Spector

Meret Oppenheim's Paris years were indelibly marked by her association with the circle of artists and poets affiliated with Surrealism. The works she created during this early period—capricious, yet macabre, line drawings; studies for sculpture; visionary poems; designs for whimsical fashion accessories; and perfectly irksome objects—were gleaned primarily from dream imagery and an unfettered imagination. The precociousness of her aesthetic sensibility exhibited innate affinities with Surrealist strategies, though she has consistently denied any calculated connection to the movement. Be that as it may, she did share an irrefutable zest for provocation and transgression with her French associates, one that endured throughout her long career.[1] Oppenheim's independent and innovative spirit is forever documented in a photographic chronicle of her sojourn in Paris. From 1933 to 1936, she posed for Man Ray's camera, appearing in sundry stylized portraits, nude studies, and a series of theatrical pictures set in the atelier of Cubist painter Louis Marcoussis. An image from this series was published in the Surrealist journal *Minotaure* in 1934 (fig. 1). Its depiction of a young, beautiful, and unclothed Oppenheim caused an absolute *succès scandaleux*, one which earned for her the dubious, yet prevalent, reputation of Surrealist "muse."

Man Ray's own published recollections of his photographic sessions with Oppenheim reflect such an attitude, confirming that the (male) Surrealists did indeed think of her as a woman first and an artist only second:

Meret was one of the most uninhibited women I have ever met. She posed for me in the nude, her hands, and arms smeared with the black ink of an etching press in Marcoussis's studio. The latter . . . wore a false beard in one of the

Fig. 1 Man Ray, untitled (Meret Oppenheim "Veiled Erotic"), 1933. Centre National d'Art et de Culture Georges Pompidou, Musée national d'art moderne, Paris.

pictures. This was a bit too scabrous for the deluxe art magazine for which it was intended; the one of Meret alone, leaning on the press, was used. Still, it was very disturbing, a perfect example of the Surrealist tendency toward scandal.[2]

While Oppenheim admitted to appreciating, in a youthful "esprit de rébellion,"[3] the uproar caused by the overtly erotic substance of the published photograph, her relegation to the role of mute, passive model by her peers (as well as by subsequent art historians) has eclipsed more complex readings of her very visible presence in the annals of Surrealism. The sensationalized reception of Oppenheim's image has overshadowed any attempt to understand how her photographic representations might relate to her overall aesthetic and theoretical project. And her own repeated renunciation of the photographs' relevance to her work as an independent artist has further hindered attempts at interpretation. However, when the actual photographic images, the context in which they were produced, and Oppenheim's own commentary about them are contemplated together, telling disparities begin to emerge that counter the artist's claim to passivity. Such is the theme of this essay.

The shock value of Oppenheim's appearance in Man Ray's photographs guaranteed her a special, though subordinate, place in André Breton's coterie. For the Surrealists, who were ever seeking unmediated access to the mythical realm of the creative unconscious, she appeared the very embodiment of their desires. Young, intelligent, uninhibited, and alluring, Oppenheim promised to fulfill their dreams of a *femme-enfant*, an "innocent" womanchild who would guide them to the furthest recesses of their minds, while simultaneously arousing their libidos.[4] Max Ernst made an oblique reference to this perception of Oppenheim as a naive libertine in the introduction he penned for her first solo exhibition at the Galerie Schulthess in Basel in 1936. In a fantastical biographical sketch, Ernst praised the artist's "freshness and charm," and then recounted an imaginary, impetuous youth:

At the age of fifteen, she leaves her father and mother to chase after half-grown trains and the most important inlets. At twenty, she locks herself into an air-crevasse and swallows the key. After a four-day fast, she suddenly breaks out and since enjoys playing—whatever for?—with the handle attachments of coastal countries and mountain foothills.[5]

In the course of this text, he referred to Oppenheim as *Meretlein* (little Meret), in a deliberate invocation of the eponymous wild child who dwells in a forest in Gottfried Keller's novel *Der Grüne Heinrich* (Green Henry). Oppenheim was actually named after this literary character—a primitive little girl dwelling alone in the forest—but its evocation by Ernst had distinct erotic overtones.[6] This correlation between Oppenheim and a free-spirited, wholly "natural" creature prevailed even after she had gained international recognition as a mature artist. In a 1970 article devoted to her work, for instance, French critic Alain Jouffroy echoed such sentiments by focusing on the Man Ray photographs and lauding her participation in them as an "act of love." He maintained that she offered her body "as a present," with an absolute purity of heart and generosity of spirit. "I admire Meret," he proclaimed, "as the most free woman who has ever existed," citing as proof that she urinated into the hat of a haughty gentleman on the terrace of the Café du Dôme and stripped off all her clothes.[7]

The Surrealists' much-touted revolution of the mind was mapped on the female body; its metaphors were erotic, its attitudes misogynist. Woman was venerated, but only inasmuch as she played the designated role—*femme-enfant*, hysteric, or muse—thought necessary to transport her male counterpart to the heights of aesthetic ecstasy. While not a Surrealist artist in her own right, Oppenheim herself was colonized as a Surrealist object: her body a territory to peruse; her art works, spoils to expropriate. In this light, it is understandable why she adamantly denied the relevance of Man Ray's photographs to her own work, claiming, in retrospect, that she saw no connection between her art and the "body of a young girl."[8] What often remains unsaid in studies of Oppenheim's early work but might help to explain her dismissal of the photography is the fact that she was intimately involved with Man Ray at the time, and perhaps, in later years resolved not to divulge such aspects of her private life. Nonetheless, it is possible to infer the dynamics of their liaison from the images themselves. A number of unpublished prints in the photographic archives of the Centre Georges Pompidou in Paris, for instance, could be regarded as "pornographic" depictions of the young artist; others are casual but intimate portraits taken in cafés and parks. With utmost discretion and, in some cases, seeming impatience, Oppenheim dismissed the experience of working with Man Ray as incidental, simply something she agreed to do out of friendship with the artist and respect for his work. She also rejected the

Fig. 2 Man Ray, untitled (Marcoussis and Meret Oppenheim), 1933. Centre National d'Art et de Culture Georges Pompidou, Musée national d'art moderne, Paris

notion that the resulting photographs, particularly the ones staged in Marcoussis's studio, were a collaborative effort between photographer and model, between older and younger artist. Stressing the point that she barely spoke French at the time, Oppenheim publically played down any connection between her own artistic objectives and those of Man Ray. In a letter to Whitney Chadwick, she explained:

When I met the group, end of 1933, I was twenty years old and not at all sure about political opinions. I made my work and did not worry about these discussions. (After the war, I met Man Ray again. He said to me: "But you are speaking!" I asked him: "Why do you say that?" He answered: "You never said a word formerly.")[9]

Oppenheim's claims to silence and her persistent refusal of agency have been often quoted and used to justify the exclusion of the photographs from her own exhibitions.[10] Be that as it may, the artist made other remarks about her experiences with Man Ray that subtly disrupt the seamlessness of her "official" account by interjecting the potential of complicity. Discussing the episode in 1981 with German critic Ingrid Strobl, she stated she was not Man Ray's model, but rather his "colleague."[11] In a subsequent interview dating from 1983, Oppenheim once again recounted how she came to pose in the nude for Man Ray because it appealed to her antibourgeois convictions. Describing the Marcoussis studio series, in which she appears near a large, lithographic printing press wearing nothing but a film of black ink on her forearm and hand, she downplayed any premeditation for this enigmatic mise-en-scène, while suggesting the possibility that the photographs were a result of spontaneous interaction between her and the photographer. She said that she was unsure where the idea of covering her arm with the ink had come from, as it was totally unrehearsed. She also explained that her mysterious smile was completely impulsive, since she found the whole situation quite amusing.[12]

Oppenheim's disavowal of the conscious agency notwithstanding, the ink stain on her arm became the leitmotif of a series of images that critically challenges the traditional view of the female body as passive witness to the artistic process. Three of the five photographs depict Oppenheim standing near the wheel of the press, prominently displaying the black smudge on her arm. Another picture shows Marcoussis—sporting a false beard—wiping the stain from her body with a white cloth (fig. 2). While the images resonate with sexual innuendo—with not-so-veiled allusions to Sadean erotica and torture—they also meta-phorically equate the photographic process, as an *imprint* of light on chemically treated paper, with the erotic references embedded in the imagery. Oppenheim appears here as a human extension of the printing press. The arching spokes of the lithographic wheel reiterate the curves of her body and, in turn, the choker around her neck echoes the cir-cumference of the circle. The ink on her arm—the substance used to produce an imprint, to inscribe meaning—makes her an integral part of the operation.[13] Her yielding posture intimates a sensual complicity with both the machinery that she touches and the camera with which she interacts. Here the printing press and the camera, both mechanized means of infinite reproducibility, conjoin with the depiction of Oppenheim as an artist at work to intimate the erotic nature of art-making so dear to the Surrealists. At the same time, this conflation of symbols offers a prototype of female creativity typically eclipsed by the masculinized model of the artistic genius.[14]

It is always treacherous to navigate retrospectively through the terrain of an artist's intentions. All too often one relies purely on conjecture and poetic license. For the sake of argument, however, the disparities in Oppenheim's own biographical account beg a certain amount of speculation as to how the photographs that she so emphatical-ly disowned might fit into her oeuvre. Previous efforts have been made to read Man Ray's pictures of the artist as a kind of "self-portraiture," in which she asserted her own subjectivity in front of the camera's objecti-fying lens.[15] The fact that Oppenheim was photographed throughout her career, often projecting a flamboyant, staged presence, suggests that this may have been the case. Her own deployment of photography in the creation of two "self-portraits"—*X-Ray of M.O.'s Skull*, 1964 (fig. 3), and *Portrait (Photo) with Tattoo*, 1980 (fig. 4)—further justifies the argument for artistic agency. It may be impossible to ascertain exactly which "self" was being offered for view in Man Ray's images, as any "self" is always an amalgamation of social personas, interior states, and gender role-playing. But in Oppenheim's case, the fact that she intentionally constructed and performed various "selves" for the camera must be regarded as an important part of her aesthetic philosophy.

The picture from the Marcoussis studio series used to illustrate Breton's essay on convulsive beauty under the title of *Erotique voilée* (Veiled Erotic) in the May 1934 issue of *Minotaure* conveys, through a sly photographic ruse, Oppenheim's insistence that art should be

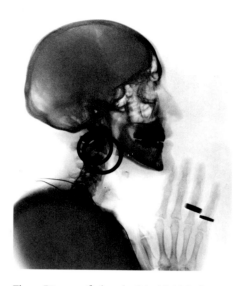

Fig. 3 *Röntgenaufnahme des Schädels M.O. / X-Ray of M.O.'s Skull*, 1964. X-ray, 10¹/₁₆ × 8⅛ in (25.5 × 20.5 cm). Galerie Renée Ziegler, Zurich

Fig. 4 *Porträt (Photo) mit Tätowierung/Portrait (Photo) with Tattoo*, 1980

"androgynous." When published, the image was cropped at torso level, showing only the upper portion of the artist's body. This editorial abbreviation omitted the essential ploy of the picture, the "secret" or "veiled" joke between Man Ray and Oppenheim. In the uncropped picture, the handle of the wheel falls exactly at groin level, bestowing the model with a protruding phallus that transforms her into a hermaphrodite. Through photographic illusion, the artist is rendered neither woman nor man, but a combination of the two. While Oppenheim's concept of artistic "androgyny" would only be articulated later in her career, particularly on the occasion of her acceptance speech for the 1974 Art Award of the City of Basel, an early allusion to the melding of genders is indeed manifest in the photograph. Familiar from a young age with the Jungian dialectic of anima and animus, and no doubt aware of the Surrealists' investment in the myth of the androgyne, Oppenheim's own interest in androgyny reflected her deliberations on the parity of the sexes and her insistence that artists of each gender must be regarded as equals.[16] In her speech, she asserted that male artists have always been able, even encouraged, to express the female aspects of their beings, but the converse has not been true for women. "A great work of literature, art, music, philosophy," she explained, "is always the product of a whole person. And every person is both male and female."[17]

Oppenheim's understanding of androgyny as a metaphor for the unification and equivalence of opposites, the holistic coupling of equal parts, differed from that of the Surrealists, who simply resurrected an age-old patriarchal trope for their own purposes. From Aristophanes's myth of a unitary, primal being split by jealous gods into two distinct parts, each destined to search for its originary other, to Ovid's tale of Hermaphroditus in the *Metamorphoses,* the androgyne has symbolized a state of completion, one in which the full measure of man (meaning male) would find expression. Even though a commingling of genders is implied by this paradigm, the classical androgyne prescribed a subordinate role for the feminine. In Ovid, for instance, it is the female figure of Salmacis, who, after praying that she never be separated from the object of her desire, loses her own identity entirely when it is subsumed into the male body of Hermaphroditus. In the traditional account of androgyny, man is rendered complete, perfected, by a union with the feminine element. The woman's sensuousness and procreative capabilities are symbolically consumed, thus rendering her perfectly superfluous in the creation of culture. This trope has a long and rich history in Western arts and letters, appearing and reappearing in many guises: from the undivided male/female beings described in Plato's *Symposium*, to the alchemical symbol of the hermaphrodite; from the modern concept of the Bachelor Machine, to the Surrealists' absorption of the feminine principle as dictated by Breton in *Arcane 17*.[18]

In her own resuscitation of the androgyny paradigm, Oppenheim assiduously and playfully avoided a model that privileged the male gender. In fact, it can be argued that in the early Man Ray photographs, her staged image deliberately destablized the patriarchal and universal-izing dimensions of the androgyne myth. Her strategy, however, was not one of simple reversal—conversely feminizing the figure—but rather one that underscored the very mutability of gender roles. In this light, it is possible to surmise that Oppenheim staged her own parodic performance for Man Ray's camera. A one-woman show, she enacted a number of distinctive theatrical characters: fragile victim, mechanical bride, cunning hermaphrodite, and artistic prodigy. To complete this picture of artistic travesty, as it were, Oppenheim appeared cross-dressed in a 1936 photograph taken by Ed Schmid (fig. 5). Wearing a man's suit and tie, with hair slicked back, she resembled a young gen-tleman dandy. The apparent ease with which she shifted from role to role and back again serves to intimate that gender itself is performa-tive, a culturally enforced construction that polarizes the sexes in the interest of the (patriarchal) status quo.[19] Her staged transvestism may be read as a subversive commentary on culturally determined sexual inequity as well as a reclaiming of the androgyne model.

Oppenheim, it seems, took great pleasure in displaying the insta-bility of prescribed identities: gender roles were worn and discarded like used costumes. In fact, throughout her career, the artist made a variety of eccentric disguises—*Yellow Mask; Mask with Tongue Sticking Out; Mask with Ornamental Scars;* and *Leaf Mask*, etc. (none illustrated)—many of which she wore to art openings and festive events. Cited earlier, the 1980 *Portrait (Photo) with Tattoo*, a black-and-white picture of Oppenheim's older and stately presence, is yet another instance of her passion for masquerade. The photographic portrait was manipulated by the artist; she stenciled a "primitive" design onto the surface of the picture, creating an ersatz "tribal" mask or tattoo across her face. This image refers back to the Marcoussis studio series, in that the motif of body staining is central to both. The taint of black print-

Fig. 5 Meret Oppenheim, 1936 (Photo: Ed Schmid)

er's ink on the model's forearm in the Man Ray photographs linked Oppenheim to the interwoven allusions to eroticism and artistic creation found in the series. In the later portrait, the tattoo design is synonymous with her own self-presentation as an artist. However, like Man Ray's early depictions of the young model, which, to some extent, can be interpreted as "self-representations," the photograph with tattoo markings was not actually taken by Oppenheim.[20] She simply coopted another photographer's picture and made it her own by embellishing the image with an ornamental mask, a veil that both conceals and reveals her purposely ambiguous identity.

In her dismantling of gender difference and the sense of hierarchy intrinsic to it—as well as the fantasy of an integrated subjective self—Oppenheim refused to render a "true" portrayal of herself. Her first oil painting, *Sitting Figure with Folded Hands* (plate 5), a self-portrait dating from 1933, the year of Man Ray's *Veiled Erotic*, depicts the artist without any identifiable gender attributes or, for that matter, any facial features at all. The image is an invitation, a challenge to the viewer to discover the "real" Meret Oppenheim, which, like all subjective "identities," is part myth, part performance, and part projection.

Notes

1 I would like to thank Jon Ippolito for his assistance with research for this essay and his careful reading of the text.

In an interview, Oppenheim stated that her work had a "surrealist" element that predated her introduction to the group in 1932. *"Je dois dire que je faisais déjà des choses classées comme 'surréalistes' avant de les connaître mais il faut dire aussi qu'ils ont été les premiers à les regarder sans les mépriser et ceci m'a fait plaisir naturellement."* (I must say that I had already made things categorized as "surrealist" before having any knowledge of the movement, but one must also say that they were the first to consider these works without scorn, and this pleased me, naturally.) Interview with Suzanne Pagé and Béatrice Parent in *Meret Oppenheim*, exhibition catalogue, Paris: Musée d'Art Moderne de la Ville de Paris, 1984, p. 13. [Unless otherwise cited, author's translation.]

2 Man Ray, *Self-Portrait*, Boston and Toronto: Little, Brown, 1963, pp. 252–53.

3 Pagé and Parent, p. 12.

4 The concept of the *femme-enfant* was introduced in the ninth issue of *La Révolution Surréaliste* (October 1, 1927) in an article entitled, "L'Ecriture Automatique." In her study of women's ambiguous role within Surrealism, Whitney Chadwick argues that the Surrealists' obsession with the *femme-enfant* (as manifest in Breton's *Nadja*) presented the most impenetrable obstacle to women artists seeking intellectual and creative agency within the movement. See Chadwick, *Women Artists and the Surrealist Movement*, Boston: Little, Brown, 1985, p. 33. For her discussion of Oppenheim as a *"femme-enfant,"* see p. 46.

5 A facsimile of the invitation and a translation of the text appear in Bice Curiger, *Meret Oppenheim: Defiance in the Face of Freedom*, trans. Catherine Schelbert, Zurich: Parkett Publishers, Cambridge, Mass.: The MIT Press, 1989, p. 29.

6 See Maureen Sherlock, "Mistaken Identities: Meret Oppenheim," in *The Artist Outsider: Creativity and the Boundaries of Culture*, ed. Michael D. Hall, et al, Washington and London: Smithsonian, 1994, p. 281. Also see Josef Helfenstein, *Meret Oppenheim und der Surrealismus*, Stuttgart: Verlag G. Hatje, 1993, pp. 34–45, for a detailed discussion of Oppenheim's personal connection to the *Meretlein* legend as well as its significance to the Surrealists' notion of the *femme-enfant*. It is also relevant to note in the context that Oppenheim and Ernst were lovers.

7 *"Elle fait un acte d'amour et offrande, le plus pur, le plus gratuit. J'admire Meret comme la femme la plus libre qui ait existé: celle qui urinait dans les chapeaux des messieurs trop diserts, à la la terrasse du Dôme. Celle qui s'exposait entièrement."* Alain Jouffroy, "Meret Oppenheim," *Opus International* nos. 19/20 (October 1970), p. 114. See also Helfenstein, op. cit., who cites Jouffroy's remarks as an example of the trivialization of Oppenheim's project (pp. 54–55).

8 *"Je ne vois pas ce que mon oeuvre a à voir avec ce corps de jeune fille."* Pagé and Parent, p. 17. Oppenheim insisted that she had not been a naive *femme-enfant*, regardless of how she might have been perceived, as she had been sexually active since the age of seventeen. See Robert J. Belton, "Androgyny: Interview with Meret Oppenheim," in *Surrealism and Women*, eds. Mary Ann Caws, et al, Cambridge, Mass. and London: MIT Press, 1991, p. 67.

9 Chadwick, *Women Artists and the Surrealist Movement*, p. 12.

10 This was the case with her large retrospective at the Musée d'Art Moderne de la Ville de Paris in 1984.

11 *"Ich liess mich von ihm fotografieren, weil er gute Bilder machte und aus Freundschaft. Ich war nicht sein Modell, sondern eine Kollegin."* Quoted from Ingrid Strobl, "Die Schöne und das Biest," *Emma: Zeitschrift für Frauen von Frauen*, no. 7 (July 1981), p. 59.

12 *"L'idea di farmi posare il braccio sull'inchiostro non so se l'aveva in mente o se gli è venuta al momento. Quanto al mio sorriso . . . nulla di misterioso, aveo trovate la situazione divertente."* Quoted from an interview with Ida Gianelli in *Meret Oppenheim*, Florence: Fratelli Alinari Editrice, 1983, p. 15. Oppenheim's comment is reminiscent of one made by Lee Miller, a photographer who worked with and posed extensively for Man Ray from 1929 to 1932. Discussing Man Ray's photographs, she explained: "There are many of them which are attributed to Man, on which I helped . . . I do not know if it was I who made them. . . . But that's of no importance . . . we were nearly the same person at work." Quoted from Chadwick, *Women Artists and the Surrealist Movement*, p. 39.

13 It is interesting to note in the context of this series that Oppenheim made monotypes of the imprint of her hand in 1959.

14 For a detailed analysis of this photograph, see Mary Ann Caws, "Ladies Shot and Painted: Female Embodiment in Surrealist Art," in *The Female Body in Western Culture: Contemporary Perspectives*, ed. Susan Rubin Suleiman, Cambridge, Mass.: Harvard University Press, 1986, pp. 276–82.

15 See Helfenstein, op. cit., pp. 52–62; Renée Riese Hubert, "From *Déjeuner en fourrure* to *Caroline*: Meret Oppenheim's Chronicle of Surrealism," in Caws, *Surrealism and Women*, pp. 40–41; Sabina Lessmann, "'Das Bewusstsein hat immer ein Lieb': Fotographische Selbstbildnisse Lee Miller (1907–1977) und Meret Oppenheim (1913–1985) und die Rolle beider als Aktmodelle Man Rays," *Frauen Kunst Wissenschaft*, Rundbrief, vol. 14 (October 1992), pp. 62–65; and Werner Hoffmann, Laudatio auf Meret Oppenheim, Art Award of the City of Berlin (Grosser Kunstpries der Stadt Berlin), Akademie der Künste, Berlin, 1982.

16 For a detailed discussion of the impact of Carl Jung's thinking on Oppenheim, see Isabel Schulz, *"Edelfuchs und Morgenröte": Studien zum Werk von Meret Oppenheim*, Munich: Verlag Silke Schreiber, 1993 pp. 56–64. For an analysis of Oppenheim's interest in androgyny, see Josef Helfenstein, "Androgynität als Bildthema und Persönlichkeitsmodell: Zu einem Grundmotiv im Werk von Meret Oppenheim," in *Meret Oppenheim Legat an das Kunstmuseum Bern*, exhibition catalogue (Kunstmuseum Bern, 1987), pp. 12–30.

17 "Acceptance Speech for the 1974 Art Award of the City of Basel, January 16, 1975," included in Curiger, op. cit., p. 130.

18 See Chadwick, op. cit., pp. 65 and 182, for a discussion of Breton's concept of androgyny.

19 The performative quality of gender is addressed in Judith Butler, *Gender Trouble: Feminism and the Subversion of Identity*, New York and London: Routledge, 1990. Though beyond the scope of this essay, Oppenheim's transvestism should also be thought through the paradigm of the libertated "New Woman" of the 1920s and 1930s, which fostered the figure of the androgyne as the ideal style for the modern, emancipated woman. See Patrice Petro, *Joyless Streets: Women and Representation in Weimar Germany*, Princeton, New Jersey: Princeton University Press, 1989, pp. 103–127.

20 The photograph was taken by Heinz Günter Mebusch of Düsseldorf in 1978. The version with stenciled tattoo was issued in an edition of fifty.

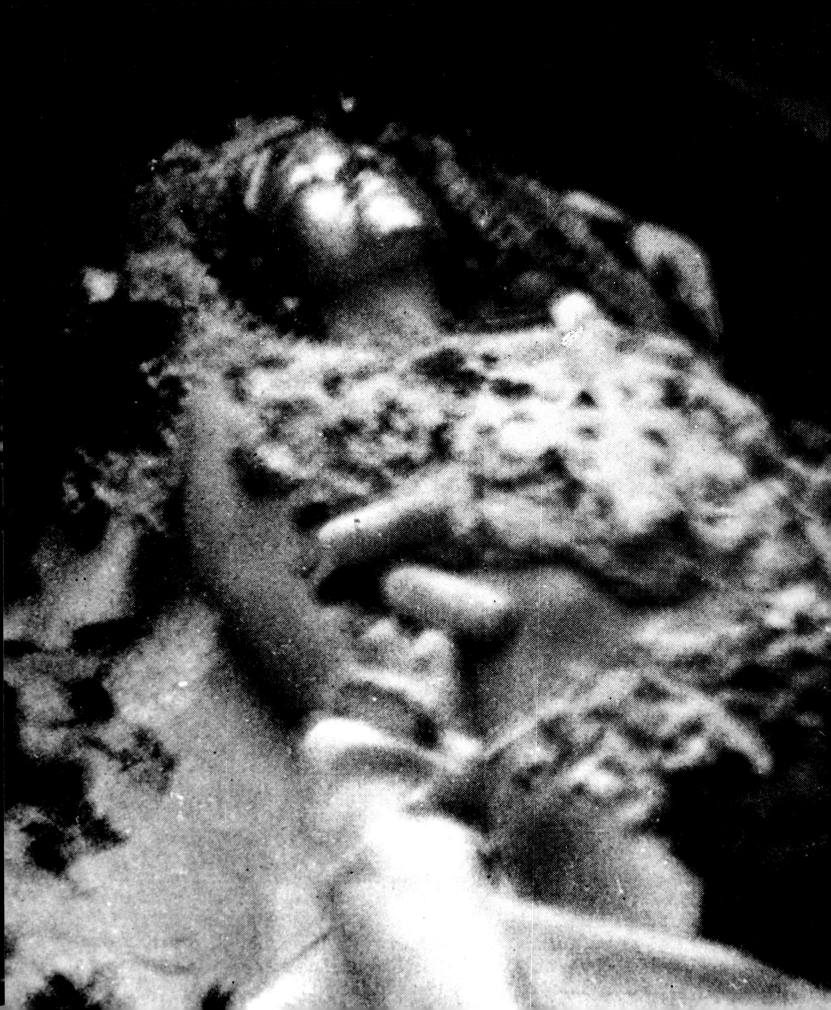

Basic Dichotomies in Meret Oppenheim's Work

Thomas McEvilley

It is amazing that Meret Oppenheim is so famous, so iconic as an artist—on the basis of a single work. Most of the world knows only the fur teacup and spoon (*Le déjeuner en fourrure / Breakfast in Fur*, 1936) (plate 15), yet on this basis alone her reputation seems at once secure in regard to her stature, and mysterious or unknown in regard to her identity. She is known or vaguely regarded as a Surrealist, and the sense of mystery that has surrounded her has probably contributed positively to this somewhat simplistic designation.

Surrealism has often been exemplified by a phrase of Isidore-Lucien Ducasse (Le Comte de Lautréamont, 1847–1870), in *Les Chants de Maldoror:* ". . . the chance meeting of a sewing machine and an umbrella on a dissecting table."[1] The famous text was first published in 1868 (though not released until 1879), and a generation or two later was discovered and taken up by Dadaists and Surrealists. Ducasse was hailed as an ancestor or precursor of Surrealism, and Man Ray, in 1920, paid homage to him in *The Mystery of Isidore Ducasse*, a sculpture that appears to be a sewing maching wrapped in a blanket.

The three objects in Ducasse's parable—so to call it—are not normally seen together. The surprise of their conjunction creates what Russian "formalist" critics called a "making strange." Reality is for the moment made strange, made anew; the world is redefined. It is no longer the place where these three things do not belong together; it is now the place where it is in fact appropriate to see them together. The nature of a reality, or of a world, has to do with one's sense of what is appropriate or natural within that reality. The vision of the umbrella and sewing machine on the dissecting table posits a different naturalness and a different world altogether.

Das Frühlingsfest / Spring Banquet, Bern, April 1959. Photograph Collection of the Photo Archive, Bern

Fig. 1 *Tisch mit Vogelfüssen/ Table with Bird's Feet*, 1939. Top: carved and gold-plated wood; feet: bronze, ca. 25 ⅝ × 27 ⁹⁄₁₆ × 19 ¹¹⁄₁₆ in (ca. 65 × 70 × 50 cm). Marian Goodman Gallery, New York

Ducasse's image does come with a certain inner definition, though it seems to attempt a state of lack of definition. The image has the effect of deconstructing existing culture by attacking its sense of the appropriate, of what goes with what. This is experienced as dangerous and threatening. Putting things together that do not go together in terms of what the society around them thinks it means is inherently threatening to intellectual, and perhaps social, order.

Ducasse built this sense of danger into his image. Two of the three objects conjoined involve the acts of cutting and piercing. The third, the umbrella, is a traditional comic instrument for striking another human. The piece is not really undefined; it flaunts its definition as a danger to society. At the same time, read iconographically, the three objects in the parable can be seen as reconstitutive: the sewing machine unites; the umbrella protects; the dissecting table has something to do with medical practice or training. A finely pointed ambiguity pervades the field—a sense of deconstructing in order to rebuild. It has also been suggested that the sewing machine, with its reference to crafts performed at home, is a female symbol, and the umbrella, with its reference to walking about in the world, not to mention its extended form, a male symbol. The image deals in a dangerous and threatening way with sexuality and its rogue relationship to social order.

Nature / Culture Contradiction

Meret Oppenheim's *Breakfast in Fur*, as in Ducasse's formula, brings together two things that are not usually encountered in tandem, but rather are regarded as inappropriate for each other's company. However, the two things conjoined inappropriately are not, as they were in the Ducasse image, devices designed for different cultural purposes. Instead, Oppenheim conjoins a cultural object with a natural condition—the condition of furry beasts—that is, nonhuman mammals which do not drink from teacups or eat from spoons. Ducasse pointed to inner contradictions within culture; Oppenheim's famous piece points to a contradiction between culture and nature. Rather than turning culture against itself through emphasizing its internal contradictions, she goes outside culture, threatening to sink it ultimately into the other. The fur grows over the teacup like fur growing on a werewolf in a horror movie. Does it become threatening and terrifying, a denial of the reality of what is regarded as human nature, an assertion that it contains the beast? Or is it a hopeful assertion to the effect that nature will ultimately somehow redeem the problems of culture? These two themes are infolded in the strangeness of the piece, its ambivalence, a question mark about human destiny. At the same time, the female/male dichotomy is focused in the conjunction of the uterine vessel and the extended spoon that enters it.

The mingling of this theme with the nature/culture theme suggests, somewhat as Sigmund Freud did in *Civilization and Its Discontents*, that it is sexual nature that binds us to the animal kingdom and threatens civilization. These themes were to intersect and interact in Oppenheim's oeuvre many times. Her classic piece is as oppositional as Ducasse's parable, but more radical or broader in import. Both are essentially programmatic; neither image is truly indefinite, though both have pretensions toward that goal. For some practitioners of Surrealism, the attempt to negate meaning was experienced as liberating and transcendent; a truly indefinite entity would in a sense transcend things with finite meanings, as an absolute is held to transcend everyday things.

Fig. 2 *Das Paradies ist unter der Erde / Paradise Is Under the Ground,* 1940

Female / Male Parallel Distinctions

Despite its strong links with Surrealism, Oppenheim's oeuvre cannot be put into that category as a whole. What will one do with *Mountains Opposite Agnuzzo (Ticino),* 1937 (not illustrated), and so many other works that seem neither deconstructive nor dangerous but earnest and aesthetically motivated? The thread of contradictory fire that rises and threatens to consume Oppenheim's oeuvre from time to time is coded—that is, meaningful.

One strain of works features the nature/culture dichotomy seen in *Breakfast in Fur. Table with Bird's Feet,* 1939 (fig. 1), for example, is a cultural object that is either revealing its true identity as nature or reverting back to a natural state. The painting *Paradise Is Under the Ground,* 1940 (fig. 2, plate 22), is a mysterious picture with many implications, one of which involves the interface between nature and culture: a piece of the sky is being lowered underground by a winch through a mortared brick well. The brick wall of the well is rigid and rectalinear, gridded—that is, culture. *Old Snake Nature,* a sculpture of 1970 (fig. 3, plate 68), shows the snake's eye peering out from within its coils atop a sack of coal. The sack is culture, trying to put its constraints around nature. But inside the apparently bagged and submissive nature the old

Fig. 3 *Die alte Schlange Natur / Old Snake Nature,* 1970

Fig. 4 *Dschungelfluss mit Einbaum oder Krokodil/ Jungle River with Pirogue or Crocodile*, 1975

snake's eye still looks out. Its moment will return, the snake's skin will shed, the bag will pop, the worm will turn.

Alongside this frequently repeated nature/culture confrontation is a parallel distinction between female and male. This often shows itself as a comparative exclusion of the theme of masculinity and a bringing of the feminine to the foreground. It is a strategy—later prominent among feminist artists in the 1970s—to simply pretend the patriarchy doesn't exist. Works like *Spring Banquet* (see page 44), a performance of 1959 in which dinner was served on the body of a nude woman, and *Genevieve* (plate 70), a sculpture of 1971 which suggests megalithic goddess icons, imply a worship of pre-Modernist cultural forms traditionally associated with the dominance of a "female" spirituality and social structure.

Representation / Abstraction Opposition

Yet another group of works seems to feature a third parallel distinction: the opposition between abstraction and representation. *Blades of Grass in the Wind*, 1964 (not illustrated), would be read by most viewers as an abstraction, except for the title, which functions in partial opposition to the image. *Jungle River with Pirogue or Crocodile*, a painting of 1975 (fig. 4, plate 84), would also most likely be "read" as an abstraction without the title. This seems a special device of Oppenheim's, to attempt to make the viewer see a piece in two ways at once. *The Secret of Vegetation*, 1972 (fig. 5, plate 73), combines abstraction and representation unapologetically, in a mixing of styles or visual languages that has become common, almost a new kind of kitsch, in post-Modernism.

These three dichotomies are prominent in Oppenheim's oeuvre: nature/culture, female/male, representation/abstraction. They are not simply features that happen to be there, but parallelisms that bestow a certain overall coherence or shape on the work at the level of iconographic content. Roughly, nature equates with the female and with representation, culture with the male and with abstraction. But the overall shape of the oeuvre is not merely a tension of dichotomies in a static situation; there is also a temporal element. The relations among these bipolar pairs shifted in a steady and appreciable way through the fifty years of Oppenheim's self-expression as an artist. In summary, the linked themes of female, nature, and representation dominated the work from about the 1930s through the 1950s, then progressively gave way to the themes of culture and abstraction. This major shift in emphasis seems to correlate with certain biograpical information.

Depressions and Their Impact

According to Bice Curiger's biographical essay[2] on Oppenheim, the artist suffered serious depression for much of her life, sometimes preventing her from working for years at a time. This period of depressions seems to have become intense in the mid-1930s and to have lasted without much letup until the mid-1950s, when various factors contributed to its lifting and her return to work and public life.

One symptom, or perhaps one condition, of Oppenheim's depressions was a feeling of being deeply betrayed by the limitation of opportunities for women in patriarchal societies. "I felt as if millennia of discrimination against women were resting on my shoulders," she wrote in 1937, when the depressions were becoming increasingly severe, "as if embodied in my feelings of inferiority."[3] Her feelings of inferiority prevented her from working and that in turn intensified the feelings of inferiority. Art-making, as a cultural activity, was the domain of the male. As this awareness became increasingly repressive to her exercise of her own talents, her production of work diminished and she retired more and more from public life. Almost forty years later, in a talk given in Basel, Oppenheim restated the theme. "As I see it," she said to the audience, "since the establishment of a patriarchy—in other words, since the devaluation of the female element—men have projected their inherent femininity, as a quality of inferior ilk, onto women."[4]

It was in this difficult period of about twenty years that Oppenheim focused on the traditional dichotomy between nature and culture in her work as an embodiment of the female/male dichotomy. But there were problems to this strategy. By associating the male with culture and the female with nature, Oppenheim was perpetuating a patriarchal system. As many feminists of the first generation of the women's movement would later do, she attempted to reverse the value hierarchy while maintaining the distinction. This was difficult, since it was a distinction that had already been characteristic of the patriarchy, in which woman had seemed the weak link, the unbeliever who could betray civilization and go over to a primitive and nature-based view-

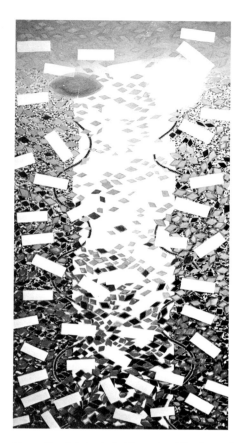

Fig. 5 *Das Geheimnis der Vegetation / The Secret of Vegetation*, 1972

Fig. 6 *Frühlingstag / Spring Day*, 1961

Fig. 7 *Die vie Elemente—Erde / The Four Elements—Earth*, 1963

point. The association of the female with nature, then, might contribute to perpetuating her oppression—and actually, it was culture she really wanted to participate in.

Again like many feminists of a later generation, Oppenheim, in her various strategies for dealing with this situation conceptually, revived notions of female identity from earlier, prepatriarchal ages. Some of her pictures, objects, and poems seem to refer directly to the idea of goddess-dominated societies or spiritualities. *Spring Day*, 1961 (fig. 6, plate 46), for example, suggests various ancient goddess icons from Chalcolithic Cyprus to what historian Maria Gimbutas called "Old Europe."[5] A femalelike biomorphic form rises as if celebrating from a tiny wire basket which may refer to the latency period of winter, or to the limitation of women in the patriarchy and their dream of breaking free.

Stone Woman, a painting of 1938 (plate 20), shows a female figure, reminiscent in its volumes of Paleolithic Venuses, lying half immersed in the ocean and half upon the land. The parts on land have turned to stone, to boulders, to pure nature; the legs, not stone-colored, but white and still in the water, are vaguely identifiable as those of a human woman. The idea of woman's closeness to nature, her tendency to slip in and out of it like a shape-changing shaman, is presented as the fundamental, indeed singular, fact in an otherwise empty landscape. But as usual, a puzzling reversal is involved. The parts of the woman or goddess that have crawled up on the shore have turned to stone; the parts that have stayed in the water are human. But the human would more often be associated with the land, and the nonhuman with the sea. There is a suggestion that woman has not yet been fully born from the womb of things, and that her ongoing attempt to force this birth is deeply problematic in some way that relates to patriarchal strictures.

Primeval Venus, 1962 (plate 52), is a sculpture in which a terracotta teepeelike structure contains straw, showing through the apex of the triangle. It evokes ancient cultures of mud, straw, and clay—of the earth. *The Four Elements—Earth,* a drawing of 1963 (fig. 7, plate 56), shows the earth element as a humanoid female in spread-legged position. Iconologists sometimes call this position the "displayed female" motif, characteristic of the neolithic period, which early feminists tended to regard as a matriarchal era. From each of her legs an evergreen tree sprouts. Her smiling face rises merrily above staring breasts. She is dynamic, creative, birth-giving.

Various poems from the same period express this theme. Characteristically, Oppenheim claims, for example, shamanic abilities to understand the languages of other species.[6] How, for example, do you find something in nature?

> *You turn the door around.*
> *You read the paeans of migrant birds, of*
> *water fishes, of damned and cursed*
> *Puẓśta beetles . . .*[7]

How will you spend your afternoon?

> *I have to write down the black words of the swans.*

And the ultimate goddess at the root of it all?

> *Anyone that sees her white fingers is ready to be*
> *transformed.*[9]

Fig. 8 *Das Paar / The Couple*, 1956

In a talk Oppenheim gave many years after the period of severe depressions had lifted, she echoed these themes. "When nature," she wrote, "has stopped being treated as the enemy of man, when the battle of the sexes has become an unknown . . . then at last, poetry and art will automatically come into their own again. . . ."[10]

It is true that when Oppenheim says nature is "treated as the enemy of man" she may be using the term *man* generically to include both men and women. Nevertheless, the fundamental accusation that the passage embodies is an accusation against patriarchy. Several of the visual works, also, seem to focus on the bondage of women, such as two sculptures of women's shoes. In *Ma gouvernante—My Nurse—mein Kindermädchen,* 1936 (plate 16), a pair of women's shoes are tied together and presented like a cooked goose on a platter. In *The Couple,* 1956 (fig. 8, plate 34), two old-fashioned, almost sadistic-looking, women's shoes are joined at the tip. Among other implications is the suggestion that women are not supposed to move; they should stand still and do what they are told. Both of these sculptures refer eerily to the traditional Chinese practice of foot-binding, which, as a Chinese guide once explained to me, was done "so they can't run away."

During this same period, while much of the work expressed this desperate nostalgia for a more female-oriented culture, other parts of the oeuvre suggested the idea of the death of nature, under the baleful influence of patriarchy. For example, as Curiger notes, *Dead Moth,* a

Fig. 9 *Toter Falter / Dead Moth*, 1946. Oil and slate on wood, 15⁹⁄₁₆ × 10¹⁄₁₆ in (39.5 × 25.5 cm). Private collection

slate sculpture of 1946 (fig. 9), is "the picture of a moth whose metamorphosis has been utterly thwarted and confined in stony rigidity."[11]

He Rocks His Wife, a painting of 1938 (plate 21), shows, in a quaint style of representation that is at once charming and chilling, a male armadillo placing his paw upon the overturned body of his mate, who lies still on her back with legs and tail as it were tucked in and taken out of action. "Is this painting," Curiger inquires, "perhaps an image of futile consolation for womanhood condemned to inactivity?"[12]

Correlation of Polarities

These two dichotomized themes—nature/culture, female/male— seem, in an overview of Oppenheim's oeuvre, to correlate to the third such polarity discussed here: representation/abstraction. Within Oppenheim's oeuvre as a whole one feels a continual tension between the down-to-earth desire to represent things as they seem to look, and a desire to abstact purer and more geometric forms from them. The classicist W. K. C. Guthrie once (at least) remarked that everyone is born either a Platonist (a worshipper of pure form) or an Aristotelian (an empiricist, more or less committed to the facts of perception). The tension between these two ideologies runs throughout Oppenheim's work as one of its inner, load-bearing walls. The aspect of her psyche that was depressed and felt inferior to men without any reason except having been brainwashed and bullied around, the aspect that retreated from a hostile patriarchal culture into nature featured representation, the thing in all its simplicity, without apparent additions of cognitive mediations that take it from the realm of perception into the realm of conception. It is true that in the early period there are some more or less abstract works, such as *Sun-bedecked Fields,* 1945 (plate 28), and that in the later period, there are examples of representation; but the emphasis and the proportions shift very dramatically.

When Oppenheim's depression began to lift in about 1954, her work seems to have changed directions, too. It progressively deemphasized the nature/culture theme and began to feature the representation/ abstraction dichotomy, which equates with it in many ways. Subsequently, her work tended more toward abstraction, though she continued her ironic practice of giving representational titles to essentially abstract works. This was yet another aspect of the gender issue, an echolike reflection of the tension between male and female, culture and nature.

Throughout the 1960s and 1970s, Oppenheim evidently felt happier, more self-confident, less wounded in ego by patriarchy. Perhaps this was because the women's movement was gaining strength, and she became a part of it.

Yet the result of a renewed sense of empowerment was, paradoxically, that in her work she veered toward abstraction, the male symbol, the symbol of culture as an enemy of nature, or vice versa. It is true that she kept representational titles on essentially visually abstract paintings, but the main thrust of her indomitable energy this time seemed toward abstraction and a sense of belonging in culture. Her commitment to nature—at least as it is embodied in the work—seems to have weakened. Her sense of participation in culture—the man's realm, according to the patriarchy—gained momentum. Her problems with "self-confidence" and "feelings of inferiority" seem to have passed. She felt confidently a part of culture's discourse and, even more, an important contributor to it.

By the time of her death in 1985, Oppenheim's work was traveling and becoming widely known as a whole. Major exhibitions in Milan, Naples, Bern, and Paris followed her participation in *documenta 7* in 1982. Increasingly, Oppenheim's oeuvre is understood as complex, multifaceted, and rightly at home in many different categories. Throughout her work, as unifying structural tensions that hold it all together in meaning, are the three great oppositional pairs that she fought with, and worked with, all her life.

Notes

1 For this translation, see Harold Szeeman and Jean Clair, editors, *Le Machina Celibi—The Bachelor Machine*, New York: Rizzoli, 1976, p. 36; for the full text, see Comte de Lautréamont, *Les Chants de Maldoror*, English translation by Guy Wernham, New York: New Directions, 1965, p. 263.

2 Bice Curiger, *Meret Oppenheim: Defiance in the Face of Freedom*, Zurich: Parkett Publishers, and Cambridge, Mass.: The MIT Press, 1989, pp. 26, 42, 61.

3 Ibid., p. 43.

4 Ibid., p. 56.

5 Maria Gimbutas, *Goddesses and Gods of Old* Europe, *7,000–3,500 B.C.: Myths, Legends and Cult Images*, Berkeley: University of California Press, 1982.

6 Of course, male poets, such as Johann Schiller (1759–1805) and Friedrich Hölderlin (1770–1843) had expressed such claims, too, but without the feminizing emphasis.

7 Curiger, p. 110.

8 Ibid., p. 111.

9 Ibid.

10 Ibid., p. 87.

11 Ibid., p. 56.

12 Ibid., p. 45.

Meret Oppenheim in the early 1980s (Photo: Nanda Lanfranco)

Plates

For you—against you

Throw all the stones behind you

And let the walls loose.

To you—on you

For one hundred singers above you

The hoofs run loose.

I delight in my mushrooms

I am the first guest in the house

And let the walls loose.   1934

1930s

l

Votivbild (Würgengel) / Votive Picture (Strangling Angel), 1931. India ink and
watercolor, 13⅜ × 6⅞ in (34 × 17.5 cm). Galerie Renée Ziegler, Zurich

2

"Für Irène Zurkinden"/"For Irène Zurkinden," 1932. Diverse materials on cardboard, 29½ × 20½ in (75 × 52 cm). Kunsthaus, Zurich

3

Skelett mit Flügeln und Palmzweig / Winged Skeleton with Palm Frond,
1933. India ink, 10⅝ × 8¼ in (27 × 21 cm). L.A.C., Switzerland

4

Dann leben wir eben später / Well, We'll Live Later Then, 1933. India ink and
gouache, 8¼ × 10⅝ in (21 × 27 cm). Collection Dominique Bürgi, Bern

5

Sitzende Figur mit verschränkten Fingern / Sitting Figure with Folded Hands, 1933. Oil on cardboard; frame by Meret Oppenheim, 11¼ × 8⅞ in (28.5 × 22.5 cm); frame: 18⁵⁄₁₆ × 15⅜ in (46.5 × 39 cm). Kunstmuseum Bern

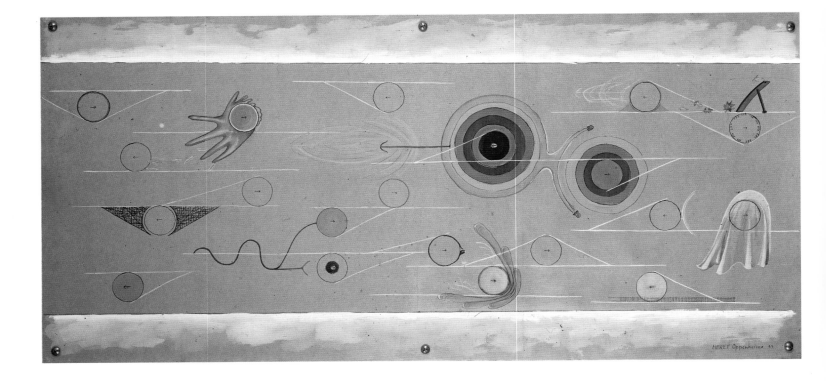

Leute auf der Strasse / People in the Street, 1933. India ink and gouache on grey cardboard, 19½ × 41⅜ in (49.5 × 105 cm). Kunstmuseum Bern

7

Husch-husch, der schönste Vokal entleert sich / Quick, Quick, the Most Beautiful Vowel Is Voiding, 1934. Oil on canvas, 17⁵⁄₁₆ × 25⁵⁄₈ in (45.5 × 65 cm).
Collection Dominique Bürgi, Bern

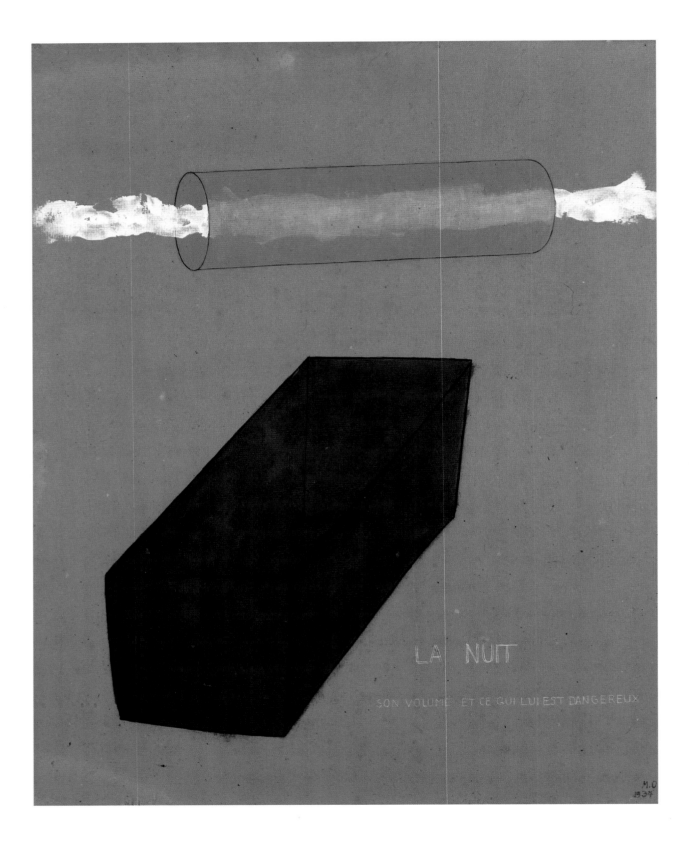

8

La nuit, son volume et ce qui lui est dangereux / The Night, Its Volume and What Endangers It, 1934. India ink and oil on grey cardboard, 31⅞ × 25⅝ in (81 × 65 cm). Private collection

9

Habillez-vous en ours blanc / Dress Up Like a Polar Bear, 1935. Oil, celluloid, and brass on cardboard, 25⅝ × 19¹¹⁄₁₆ in (65 × 50 cm). Galerie Renée Ziegler, Zurich

10

Weisser Kopf, blaues Gewand / White Head, Blue Garment, 1935. Oil, wood, and plaster relief on wood, 26¹³⁄₁₆ × 19⅞ × 4¾ in (68 × 50 × 12 cm).
Oeffentliche Kunstsammlung Basel, Kunstmuseum, Permanent loan of "Verein der Freunde des Kunstmuseums"

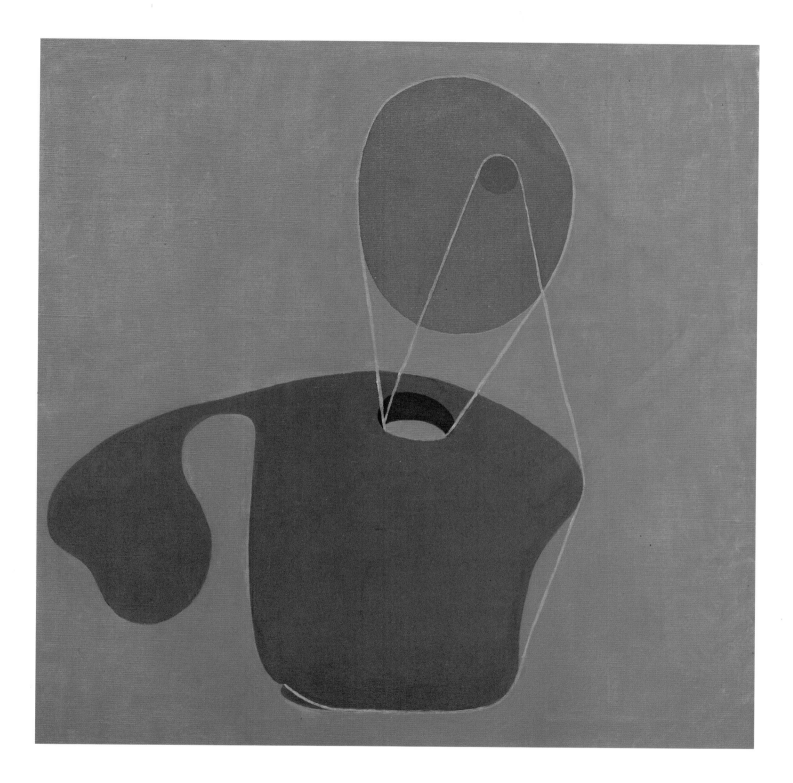

22

Roter Kopf, Blauer Körper / Red Head, Blue Body, 1936. Oil on canvas, 31½ × 31½ in (80 × 80 cm). The Museum of Modern Art, New York. Meret Oppenheim Bequest. © 1996, The Museum of Modern Art, New York

Trois poires noires / Three Black Pears, 1935 or 1936. Oil on canvas; semicircular frame by Meret Oppenheim, 15⁹⁄₁₆ × 22¹⁄₁₆ in (39.5 × 56 cm). Kunstmuseum Bern

13

Design for cape, ca. 1936. Ink and gouache, 10⅝ × 5¹⁵⁄₁₆ in (27 × 15.2 cm).
Birgit and Burkhard Wenger, Basel

14

Design for necklace, 1936. Pencil, ink, and watercolor, 6⁵⁄₁₆ × 5⅛ in
(16 × 13 cm). Birgit and Burkhard Wenger, Basel

Object (Le déjeuner en fourrure), 1936. Fur-covered cup, saucer, and spoon; cup, 4⅜ in (11 cm) diameter; saucer, 9⅜ in (24 cm) diameter; spoon: 8 in (20 cm) in length; overall height 2⅞ in (7.3 cm). The Museum of Modern Art, New York. Purchase. Photograph © 1996, The Museum of Modern Art, New York

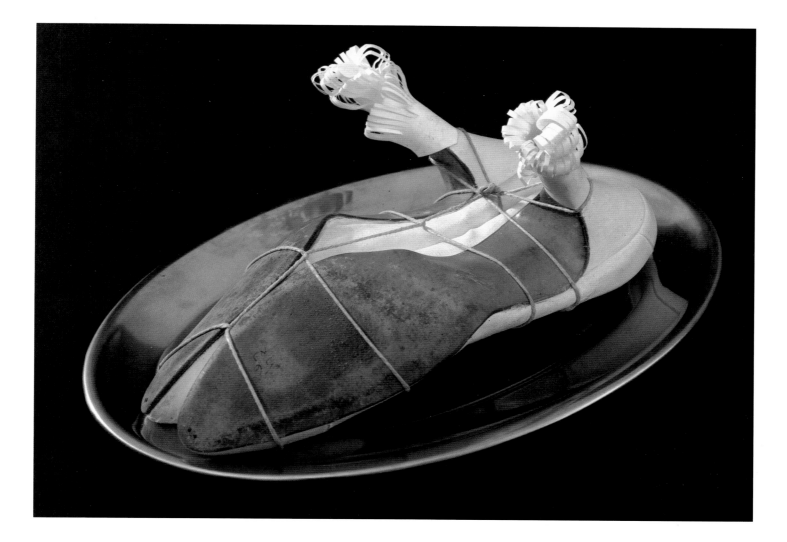

Ma gouvernante—My Nurse—mein Kindermädchen, 1936. High-heeled shoes with paper ruffles on an oval platter, 5½ × 8½ × 13 in (14 × 21 × 33 cm).
Nationalmuseum, SKM, Stockholm

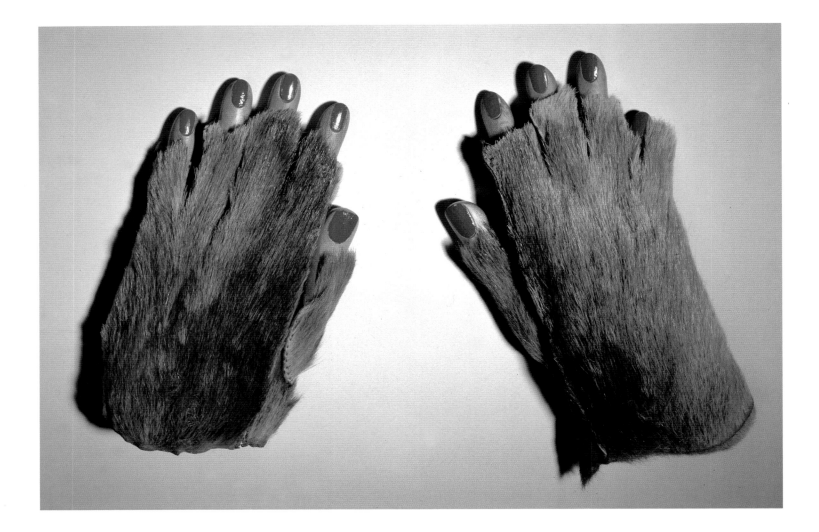

27

Fur Gloves with Wooden Fingers, 1936. Fur gloves with wooden fingers in a Plexiglas box, 2 × 4 × 8¼ in (5 × 10 × 21 cm) each; box: 19¹¹/₁₆ × 19¹¹/₁₆ × 19¹¹/₁₆ in (50 × 50 × 50 cm). Galerie Hauser & Wirth AG, Zurich

Drei Mörder im Wald / Three Murderers in the Woods, 1936. Gouache, 8½ × 8¹¹⁄₁₆ in (21.5 × 22 cm). Galerie Renée Ziegler, Zurich

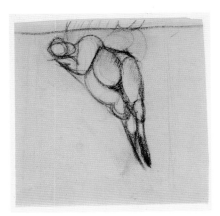

19

Steinfrau / Stone Woman, 1937. Charcoal, 6½ × 6⅞ in
(16.5 × 17.5 cm). The Menil Collection, Houston

20

Steinfrau / Stone Woman, 1938. Oil on cardboard, 23¼ × 19⁵⁄₁₆ in (59 × 49 cm).
Private collection

Il berce sa femme / He Rocks His Wife, 1938. Oil on cardboard, 2¾ × 5¾ in (7 × 14.5 cm). Private collection

Loyal captain

Tell me

Show me the place in the clouds

That the wing of the swallow opened

The valley of waves in the goddess' hair

The green lights in the forest.

Here it is night—

Evil brooms kill the kobolds

No wheel turns anymore.

Darkness does not know itself

Nor does it ask

It is a fist within a fist

That no one sees.   1944

1 9 4 0 s

22

Das Paradies ist unter der Erde / Paradise Is Under the Ground, 1940. Collage and gouache, 8¹¹⁄₁₆ × 6½ in (22 × 16.5 cm). Private collection, Hamburg

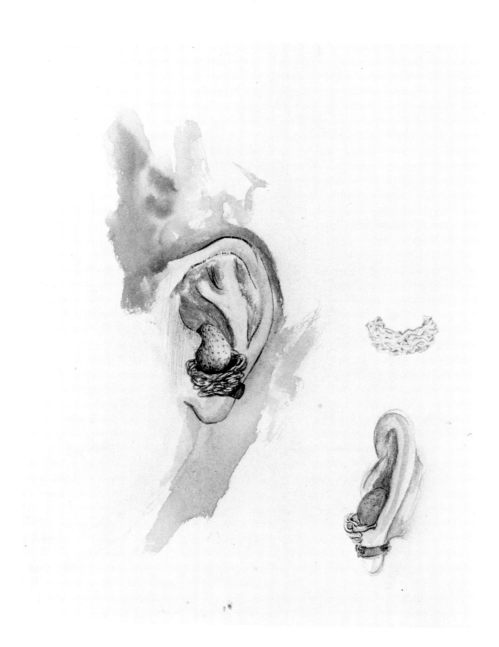

23

Design for ear decoration, 1942. Pencil and watercolor, 8¾ × 6⅝ in (22.1 × 16.8 cm). Birgit and Burkhard Wenger, Basel

24

Sonne, Mond und Sterne / Sun, Moon, and Stars, 1942. Oil on canvas, 18⅞ × 20⅛ in (48 × 51 cm). Collection Dominique Bürgi, Bern

25

Krieg und Frieden / War and Peace, 1943. Oil on canvas, 31½ × 55⅛ in (80 × 140 cm). Oeffentliche Kunstsammlung Basel, Kunstmuseum. Permanent loan of "Verein der Freunde des Kunstmuseums"

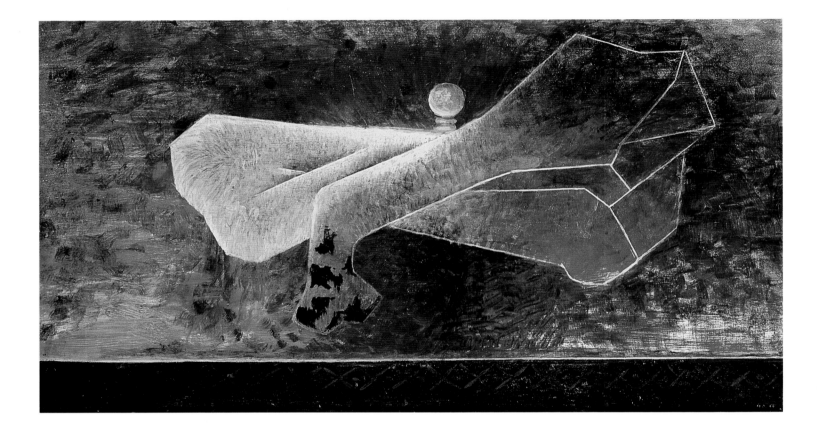

26

Das Tragikcomische / The Tragicomic, 1944. Oil on fiberboard, 15⅜ × 27⁹⁄₁₆ in (39 × 70 cm). Whereabouts unknown

Hornisse und Hummel / Hornet and Bumblebee, 1945. Oil on cardboard, 5½ × 9¼ in (14 × 23.5 cm). Private collection

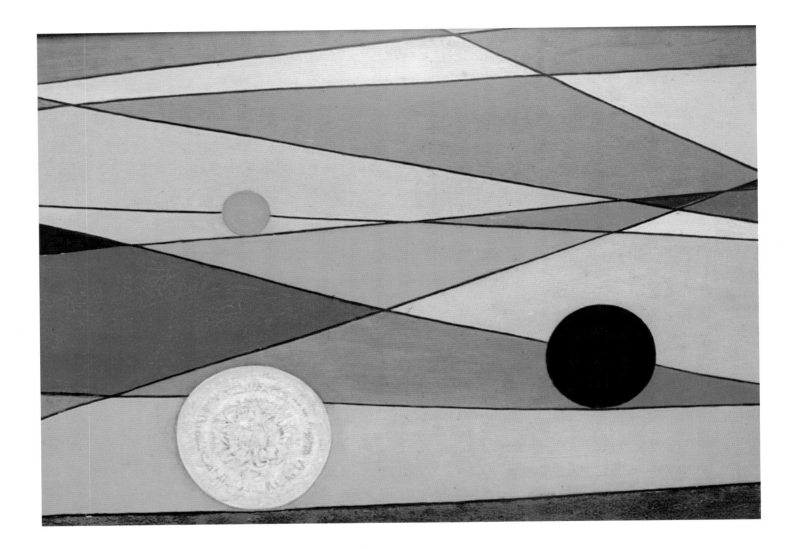

28

Besonnte Felder/ Sun-bedecked Fields, 1945. Oil on fiberboard, 19¹¹⁄₁₆ × 27⁹⁄₁₆ in (50 × 70 cm). Museo Cantonale d'arte Lugano

Nachthimmel mit schwarzen Wolken / Night Sky with Black Clouds, 1946. Oil on fiberboard, 19¹¹/₁₆ × 27⁹/₁₆ in (50 × 70 cm). Whereabouts unknown

30

Antilope mit Sonne auf dem Rücken / Antelope with Sun on Its Back, 1949. Gouache, 9¹¹⁄₁₆ × 13¼ in (24.5 × 33.5 cm).
Private collection

Baum, Schwarzspecht und Sommerwolken / Tree, Woodpecker, and Summer Clouds, 1949. Pencil and gouache, 26¹³⁄₁₆ × 20⁵⁄₁₆ in (68 × 51.5 cm). Kunstmuseum Bern

Forsaken, forgotten—

So black on the shore of oats.

I do not want to measure the time

That invented this pain.

The yellow waves cut

The new net in two.

They come, go and say:

The poor miscellany! 1936

1950s

32

Sterben in der Nacht / Dying at Night, 1953. Gouache, 19¹¹⁄₁₆ × 22¹⁄₁₆ in (50 × 56 cm). Centre Georges Pompidou, Musée national d'art moderne, Paris

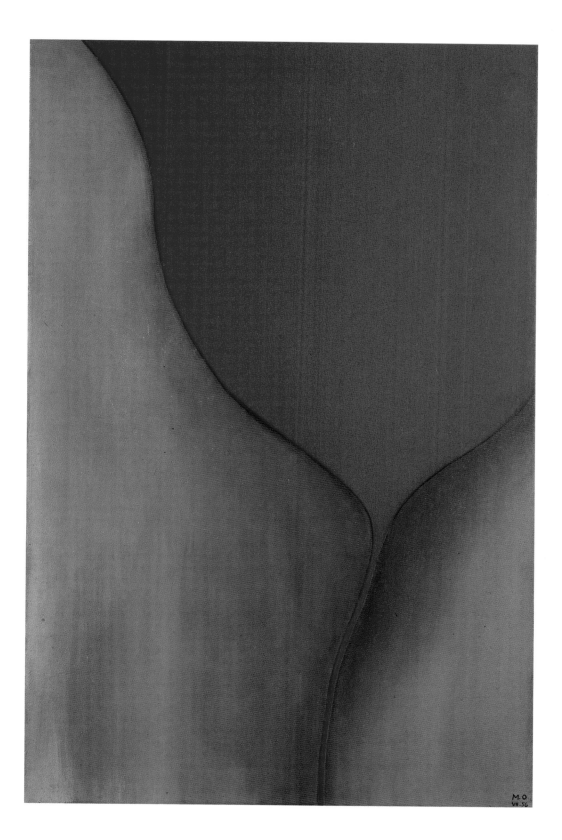

33

Das Blut des Gestirns / The Blood of a Star, 1956. Oil on canvas, 34⅝ × 22½ in (88 × 57 cm). Galerie Renée Ziegler, Zurich

Das Paar / The Couple, 1956. Pair of brown boots attached at the toes, ca. 7⅞ × 15¾ × 5¹⁵⁄₁₆ in (ca. 20 × 40 × 15 cm). Private collection

35

Sommernacht / Summer Night, 1957. Cardboard, paper and plastic disks, red (clay) stone, wire, white plastic bead, and wood frame, 5⅜ × 5⅜ in (13.5 × 13.5 cm) including frame. Private collection

36

Maskierte Blume / Masked Flower, 1958. Limewood and gouache, 42½ × 21¼ × 15¾ in (108 × 54 × 45 cm). Kunsthaus, Zurich

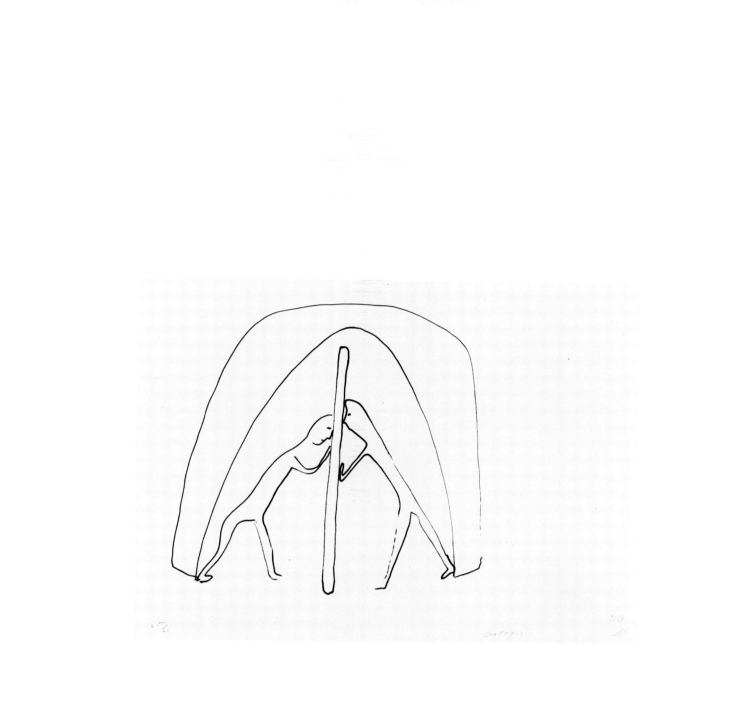

Dialog / Dialogue, 1958. India ink, 12⅝ × 16¹⁵⁄₁₆ in (32 × 43 cm). Kunstmuseum Bern

38

Berggeiſt / Mountain Spirit, 1958. Stone chips on cement core, 12⅝ × 6⅞ in (32 × 17.5 cm). Birgit and Burkhard
Wenger, Basel

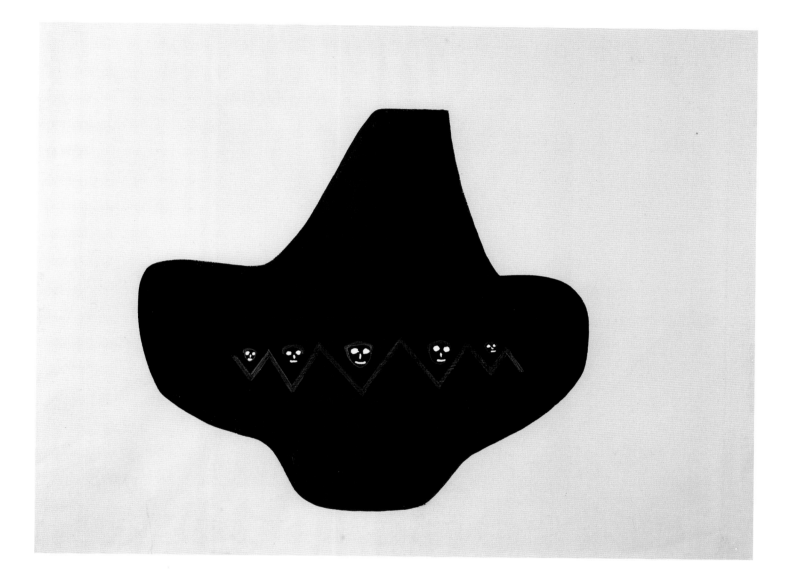

39

Schwarze Form mit Totenköpfchen / Black Shape with Little Skulls, 1959. Gouache on paper, 18⅞ × 25¼ in (48 × 64 cm). Fondazione Marguerite Arp, Locarno

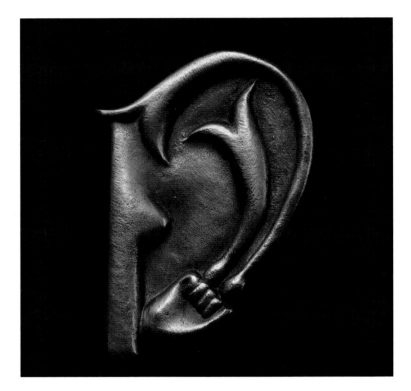

Das Ohr von Giacometti / Giacometti's Ear, 1959. Bronze, 4⁵⁄₁₆ × 3 × ⅝ in (11 × 7.5 × 1.5 cm).
Collection Dominique Bürgi, Bern

41

Der grüne Zuschauer / The Green Spectator, 1959. Limewood, oil, and sheet copper, 67¹¹⁄₁₆ × 20½ × 19¹¹⁄₁₆ in (172 × 52 × 50 cm). Kunstmuseum Bern

Up there in that garden

There stand my shadows

That cool my back.

They stand in that garden

They fight about old bread

And crow like cockerels.

Today I want to visit them

Today I want to greet them

And count their noses.   1943

1960s

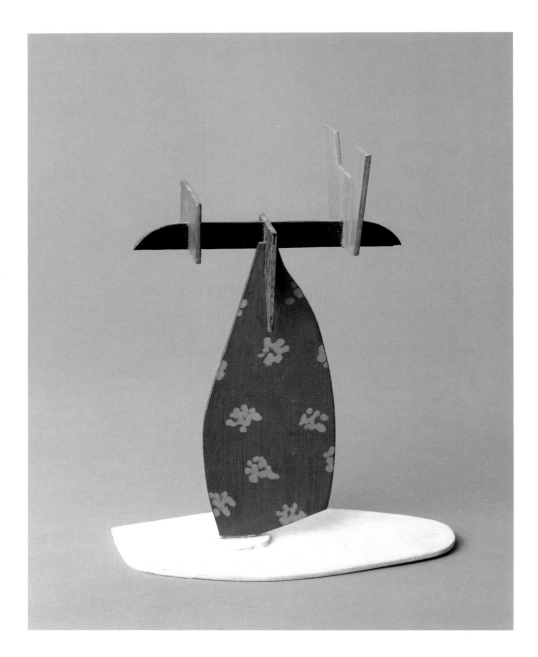

42

Bauernfrau, auf dem Kopf einen Korb tragend / Peasant Woman Carrying a Basket on Her Head, 1960. Painted wood,
9⅞ × 3¹³⁄₁₆ × 7⅞ in (25 × 8 × 20 cm). Kunstmuseum Bern

43

Schwarze Strich-Figur vor Gelb / Black Stick Figure on Yellow, 1960–81. Oil on canvas, 29$\frac{15}{16}$ × 22$\frac{7}{8}$ in (76 × 58 cm). Galerie Renée
Ziegler, Zurich

44

Eichhörnchen / Squirrel, 1960. Beer glass, fur, and plastic foam, ca. 8¹¹⁄₁₆ × 7½ in (22 × 19 cm). Galerie Renée Ziegler, Zurich

45

Der Rabe / The Raven, 1961. Oil on wood, relief of molded substance and fungus, 32½ × 11⁷⁄₁₆ × 3 in (82.5 × 29 × 9 cm). Private collection, Switzerland

Frühlingstag / Spring Day, 1961. Molded substance, wood, wire basket, and oil, 19¹¹⁄₁₆ × 13⅜ in (50 × 34 cm).
Private collection

47

Tierköpfiger Dämon / Animal-headed Demon, 1961. Neoclassical clock-case, silver-coated wood, ceramic buttons, 23¼ × 13¹³⁄₁₆ × 17¾ in (59 × 35 × 45 cm). Collection Onnasch, Berlin

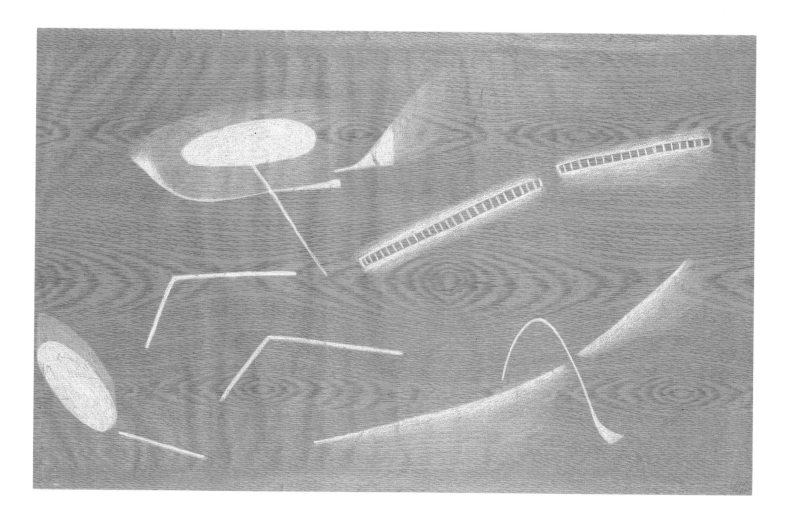

48

Die Heinzelmännchen verlassen das Haus / The Elves Leave the House, 1961. Crayon on imitation-wood paper, 21¼ × 31½ in (54 × 80 cm). Galerie Renée Ziegler, Zurich

49

Das Haus der Fee / The Fairy's House, 1961. Painted wooden stick, doll's shoe, Plexiglas box, and gilded snail's shell;
height: 15¾ in; box: 6⁵⁄₁₆ × 4¾ × 3³⁄₁₆ in (16 × 12 × 8 cm). Whereabouts unknown

50

Baumwurzeln / Roots of Trees, 1962. Charcoal and red ocher, 13¹³⁄₁₆ × 19¹¹⁄₁₆ in (35 × 50 cm). Kunstmuseum Bern

51

Miss Gardenia, 1962. Plaster in metal frame with metallic paint, 10⅝ × 6 × 4¼ in (27 × 15.3 × 10.8 cm). San Francisco Museum of Modern Art. Helen Crocker Russell Memorial Fund Purchase

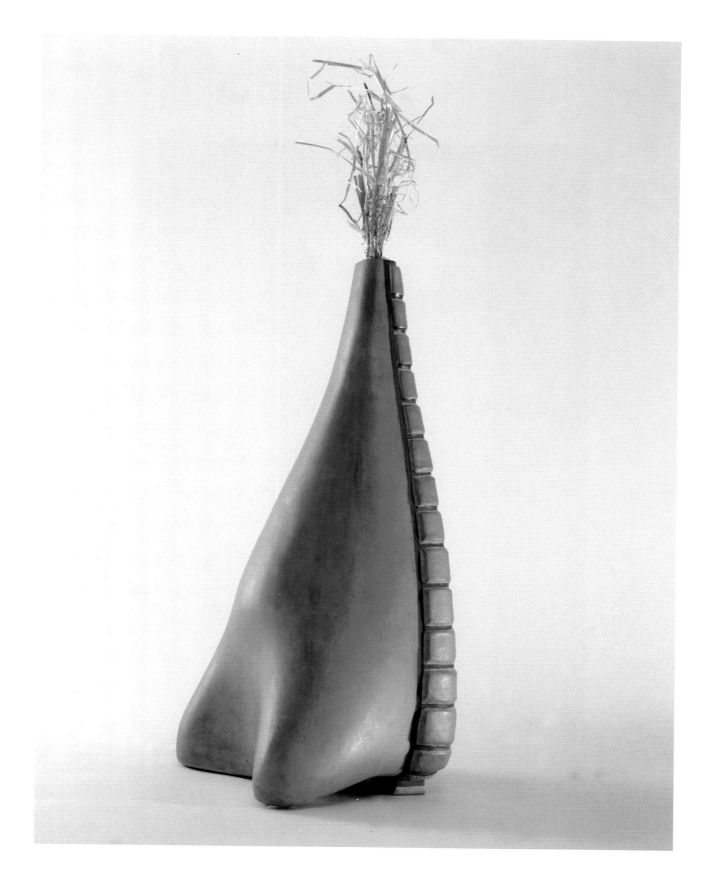

Urzeit-Venus / Primeval Venus, 1962. Terra-cotta, oil, and straw, 20⅞ × 10¼ × 7½ in (53 × 26 × 19 cm). Kunstmuseum Solothurn, Switzerland

53

Wolke auf Brücke / Cloud on Bridge, 1963. Molded substance on wooden core with oil, 18⅞ × 9¹⁄₁₆ × 5⅛ in (48 × 23 × 13 cm). Kunstmuseum Bern

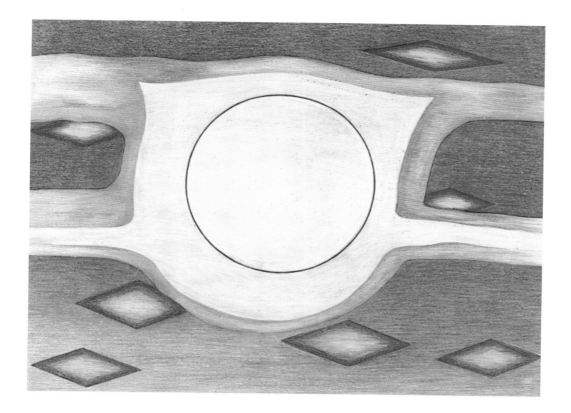

54

Sonne in Abendwolken / Sun in Evening Clouds, 1963. Crayon,
19¹¹⁄₁₆ × 25⅝ in (50 × 65 cm). Swiss Reinsurance Company, Zurich

55

Gesicht im Teich / Face in the Pond, 1963. Crayon, 19⁵⁄₁₆ × 25⁷⁄₁₆ in (49 × 64.5 cm).
Private collection

56

Die vie Elemente—Erde / The Four Elements—Earth, 1963. Pencil and colored pencil, 11¹³⁄₁₆ × 16⅜ in (30 × 41.5 cm). Kunstmuseum Bern

57

Profil / Profile, 1964. Molded substance on wood, colored chalk, oil, glass beads, and frame, 16⁹⁄₁₆ × 13⅜ in (42 × 34 cm). Private collection

58

Unter der Regenwolke / Under the Raincloud, 1964. Oil on wood and relief of molded substance, 43⁵⁄₁₆ × 29⅛ in (110 × 74 cm).
Kunstmuseum Bern

59

Das Haus an der Brücke / The House at the Bridge, 1964. Molded substance and oil on cardboard; 12¾ in (32 cm) diameter; 3³⁄₁₆ (8 cm) deep. Collection Matta, Paris

60

Die Hand (Turm) / Hand (Tower), 1964–82. Model for sculpture: Relief on canvas, Styrofoam, molded substance, and oil, 98⁷⁄₁₆ × 39⅜ × 3 in (250 × 100 × 8 cm). Kunstmuseum Bern

61

Le bouclier du chef / The Chieftain's Shield, 1965. Oil on canvas, 68⅞ × 39⅜ in (175 × 100 cm).
Private collection

62

In einer Staubwolke (die schöne Afrikanerin) / In a Cloud of Dust (The Beautiful African Woman), 1965. Oil on canvas, 55⅛ × 44½ in (140 × 113 cm). Private collection, Basel

63

Schwarzer Kamin / Black Chimney, 1966. Oil on wood, 10⅞ × 7⁵⁄₁₆ in (27.5 × 18.5 cm).
Private collection

Autoportrait et esquisse biographique depuis l'an 60 000 a.C.

64

Selbstporträt und curriculum vitae seit dem Jahr 60,000 a.C. / Self-portrait and Curriculum Vitae Since the Year 60,000 B.C., 1966. India ink, 13¹³⁄₁₆ × 9¼ in (35 × 23.5 cm). Kunstmuseum Bern

65

Bon appétit, Marcel! (Die weisse Königin) / Bon appétit, Marcel! (The White Queen), 1966. Baked dough chess queen with spine of partridge,
plate, fork, and knife, on an oilcloth chessboard, 12⅝ × 12⅝ × 1¹³⁄₁₆ in (32 × 32 × 3 cm). Collection Foster and Monique Goldstrom, New York

66

Wagen 34 / Wagon 34, 1969. Wood, lower half covered with velvet; upper half painted in oil,
29½ × 21¹¹⁄₁₆ × 3 in (75 × 55 × 8 cm). Private collection

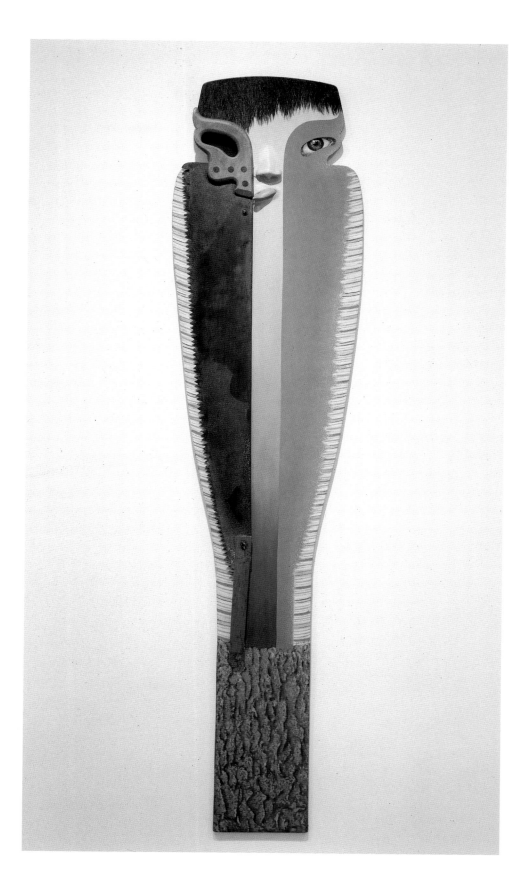

67

Oktavia / Octavia, 1969. Oil on wood, molded substance, and saw, 73⅜ × 18½ in (187 × 47 cm). Collection Amada Segarra

Finally!

Freedom!

The harpoons fly.

The rainbow is floating in the streets,

Only overshadowed by the distant humming of the giant bees.

Everyone loses everything, which they, oh so often,

Have overflown in vain.

But:

Genevieve:

Stiff

Standing on her head

Two meters above the ground

Without arms.

Her son Realm of Pain:

Wrapped into her hair.

Small fountain.

I repeat: small fountain.

Wind and cries in the distance.   1933

1970s

68

Die alte Schlange Natur / Old Snake Nature, 1970. Snake, anthracite on wire; sheep's head, modeled out of Rugosit, filled and painted in oil; sack filled with rising clay, 27⁹⁄₁₆ × 20½ × 21¹¹⁄₁₆ in (70 × 52 × 55 cm). Centre Georges Pompidou, Musée national d'art moderne, Paris

69

Andenken an das Pelzfrühstück / Souvenir of Breakfast in Fur, 1970. Cup and spoon of imitation fur and imitation damask under raised glass, 7⅞ × 6¹¹⁄₁₆ × 2 in (20 × 17 × 5 cm). Galerie Renée Ziegler, Zurich

70

Genoveva / Genevieve, 1971. Wooden board, two poles and oil, 50⅜ × ca. 47¼ × 29⅛ in (128 × ca. 120 × 74 cm).
Museum moderner Kunst Stiftung Ludwig, Vienna

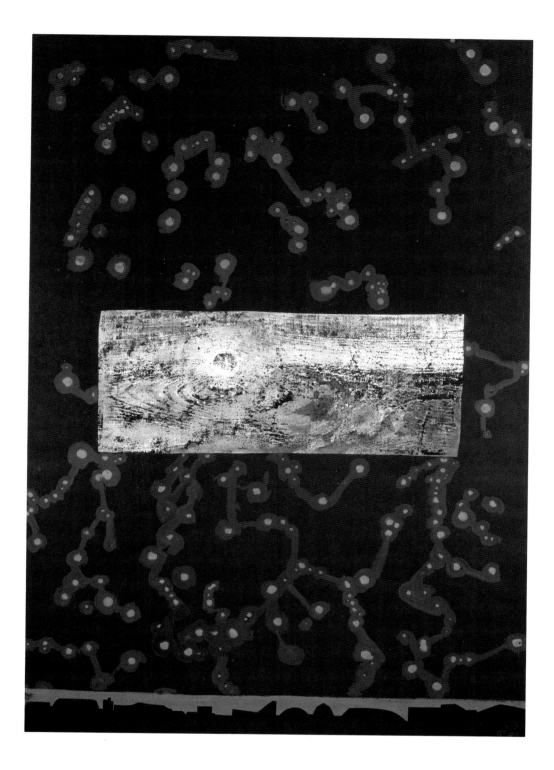

Gestirnter Himmel und Sonnenuntergang / Starry Skies and Sunset, 1971. Gouache and lithotint on photographer's black cardboard, 39⅜ × 27⁹⁄₁₆ in (100 × 70 cm). Galerie Renée Ziegler, Zurich

Die Spirale (der Gang der Natur) / Spiral (Nature's Way), 1971. Plaster model with four "heads" of movable glass, painted in oil on plaster base, 11¹³⁄₁₆ × 4¹⁵⁄₁₆ × 4¹⁵⁄₁₆ in (30 × 12.5 × 12.5 cm); base: 5⅞ × 5⅞ × 5⅞ in (15 × 15 × 15 cm). French Ministry of Culture, Paris

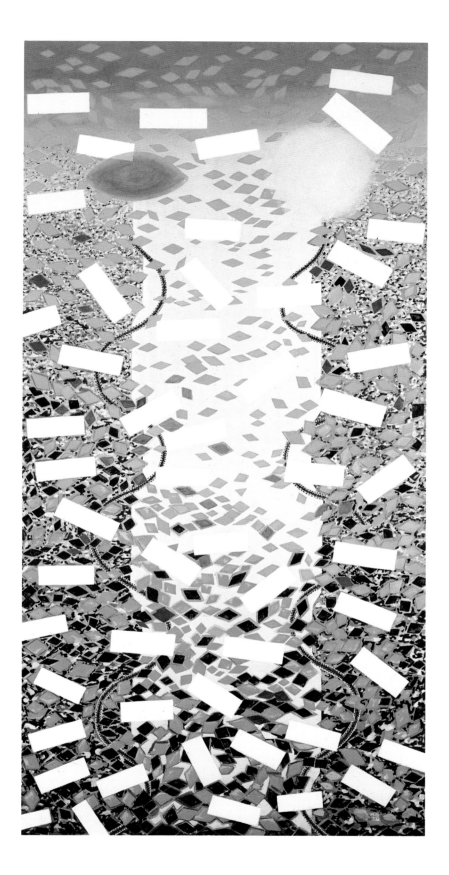

Das Geheimnis der Vegetation / The Secret of Vegetation, 1972. Oil on canvas, 76¾ × 38 ³⁄₁₆ in
(195 × 97 cm). Kunstmuseum Bern

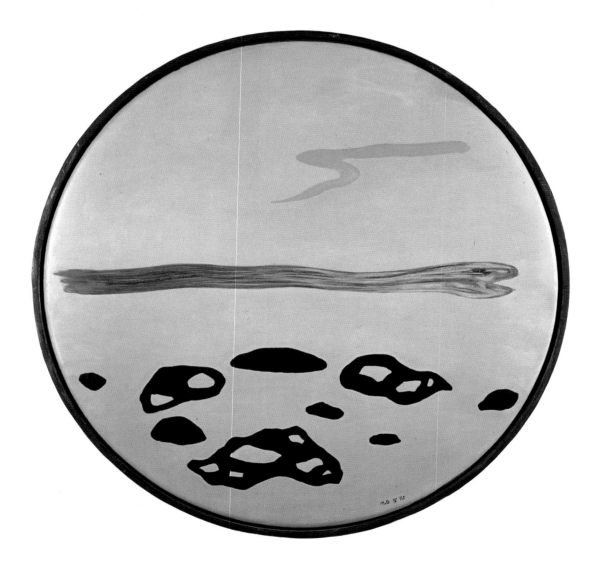

Schlange und schwarze Steine / Snake and Black Stones, 1972. Oil on plastic drumhead, 22⅞ in (58 cm) diameter. Kunstmuseum Solothurn, Switzerland

75

Ein Abend im Jahre 1910 / An Evening in the Year 1910, 1972. Oil on fiberboard with imitation tiles, 19¹¹⁄₁₆ × 25⅝ in (50 × 65 cm). Kunstmuseum Bern

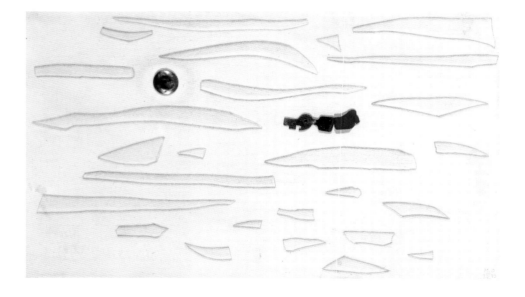

76

Fliegender Hund / Flying Dog, 1973. Colored pencil and pasted objects,
11¹³⁄₁₆ × 19¹¹⁄₁₆ in (30 × 50 cm). Private collection, Bern

77

Spirale—Schlange im Rechteck / Spiral—Snake in Rectangle, 1973.
Crayon, 26¹³⁄₁₆ × 19½ in (68 × 49.5 cm). Kunstmuseum Bern

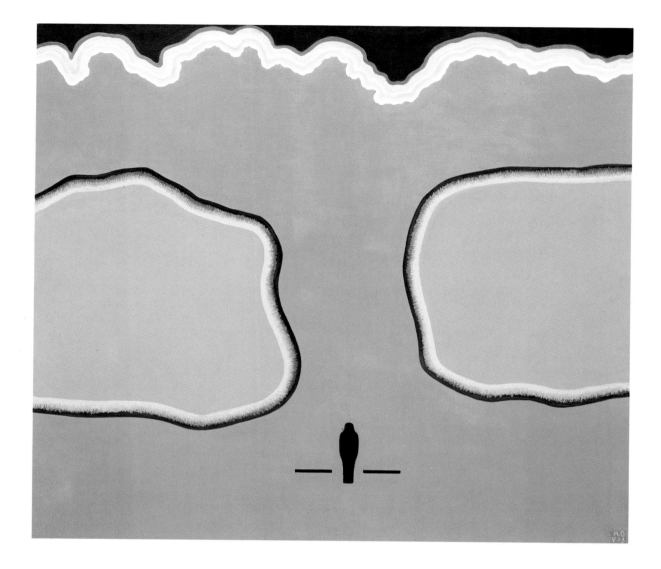

La condition humaine / Man's Fate, 1973. Oil on canvas, 35⁷⁄₁₆ × 39⅜ in (90 × 100 cm). Collection David Bowie

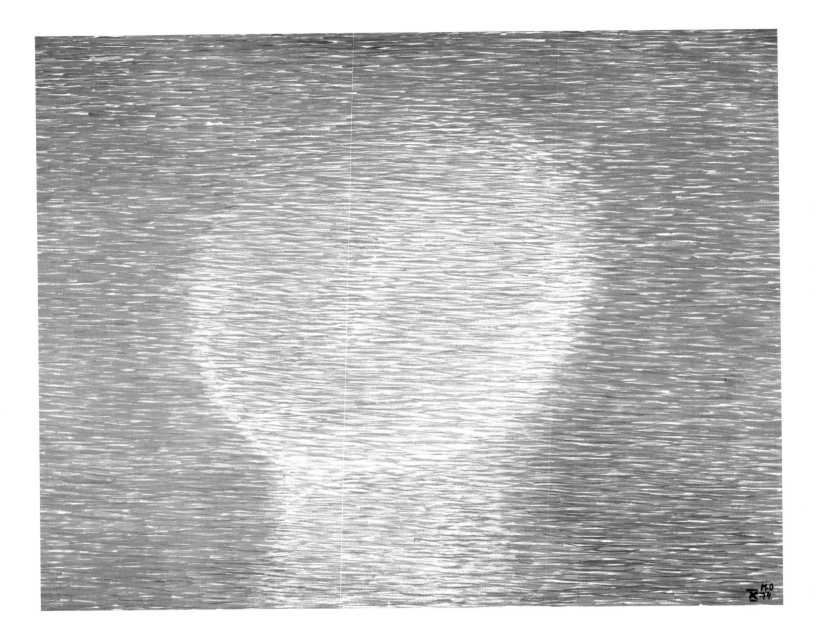

79

Nebelkopf / Head of Fog, 1974. Oil on canvas, 25⅝ × 31⅞ in (65 × 81 cm). Kunstmuseum Bern

Verborgenes im Nebel / Hidden in the Fog, 1974. Oil on canvas, 39⅜ × 31⅞ in (100 × 81 cm). Swiss Mobiliar Insurance Company, Bern

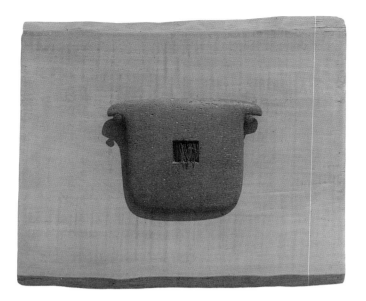

81

Der Eingang / The Entrance, 1974. Stone, curtain, and pearls on board, 10½ × 13 × 1³⁄₁₆ in (26.5 × 33 × 3 cm); board, 24⁷⁄₁₆ × 28⅜ in (62 × 72 cm). Fundación Yannick y Ben Jakober, Mallorca

82

Das Messer / Knife, 1975. Glass splinters, hemp, and painted buttons on a butcher's knife, 12⅝ × 5⅛ × ⁹⁄₁₆ in (32 × 13 × 1.5 cm). Kunstmuseum Bern

83

Gesicht-Insekt / Face Insect, 1975. Wax, feathers, and wood, 21¹¹⁄₁₆ × 17¾ × 4⁵⁄₁₆ in (55 × 45 × 11 cm). Private collection

84

Dschungelfluss mit Einbaum oder Krokodil / Jungle River with Pirogue or Crocodile, 1975. Oil on canvas and worm-eaten wood, 25¼ × 34⅝ in (64 × 88 cm). Collection
Jacques and Marion Richter, Switzerland

85

Dort fliegt sie, die Geliebte / There She Flies, the Beloved, 1975. Rugosit relief on plastic with oil, 28 × 39 in (71 × 99 cm). Gesellschaft der Freunde des Kunstmuseum Olten

86

Geier und gelb-roter fliegender Gegenstand / Vulture with Yellow and Red Flying Object, 1975.
Watercolor, colored ink, and colored chalk, 10¼ × 13⅜ in (26 × 34 cm). Private collection

87

Der Traum von der weissen Marmorschildkröte mit Hufeisen an den Füssen / The Dream of the White Marble Turtle with Horseshoes on Its Feet, 1975. Gouache and objects on paper, 14¾ × 9¹¹⁄₁₆ in (37.5 × 24.5 cm). Kunstmuseum, Lucerne

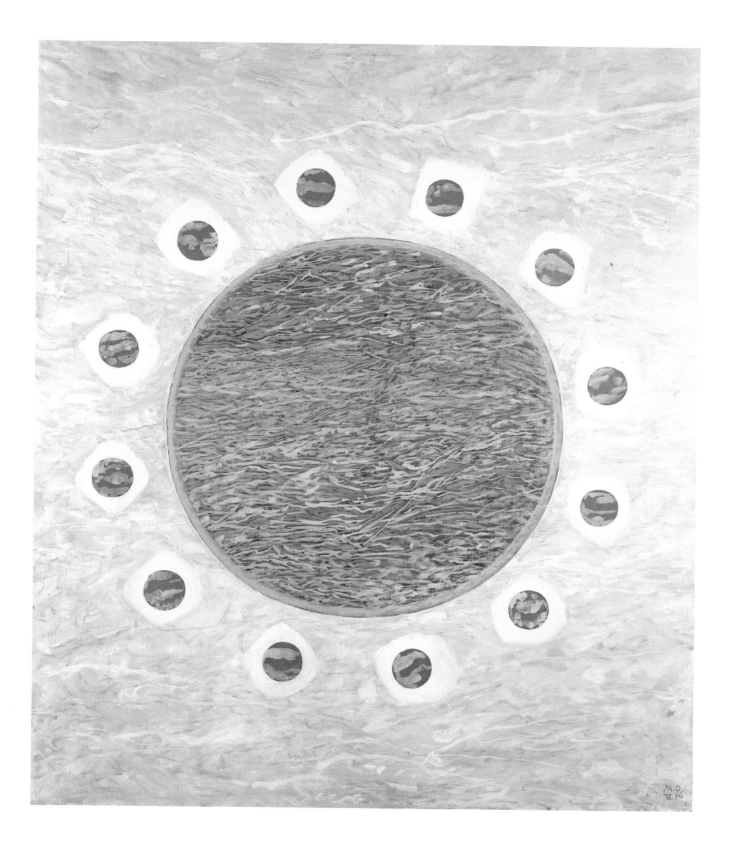

Gestirn, von zwölf Planeten umkreist / Star Circled by Twelve Planets, 1976. Oil on canvas, 37⅜ × 31½ in (95 × 80 cm). Swiss Reinsurance Company, Zurich

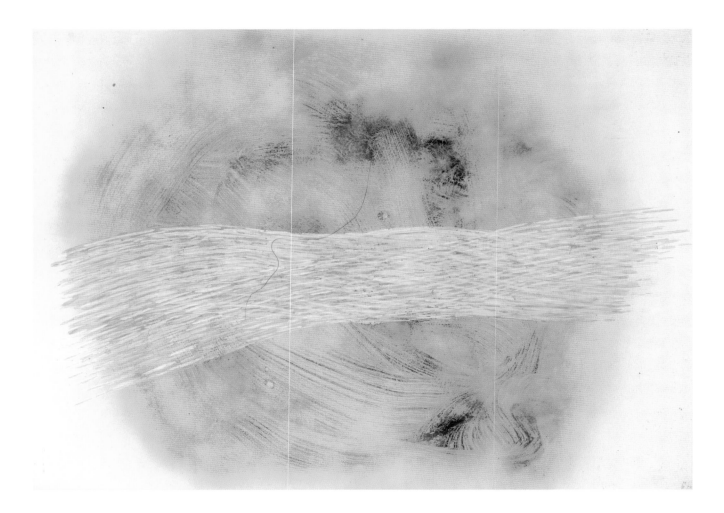

Planetenbahn / Planet's Orbit, 1976. Gouache and acrylic, 28 × 39⅜ in (71 × 100 cm). Kunstmuseum Bern

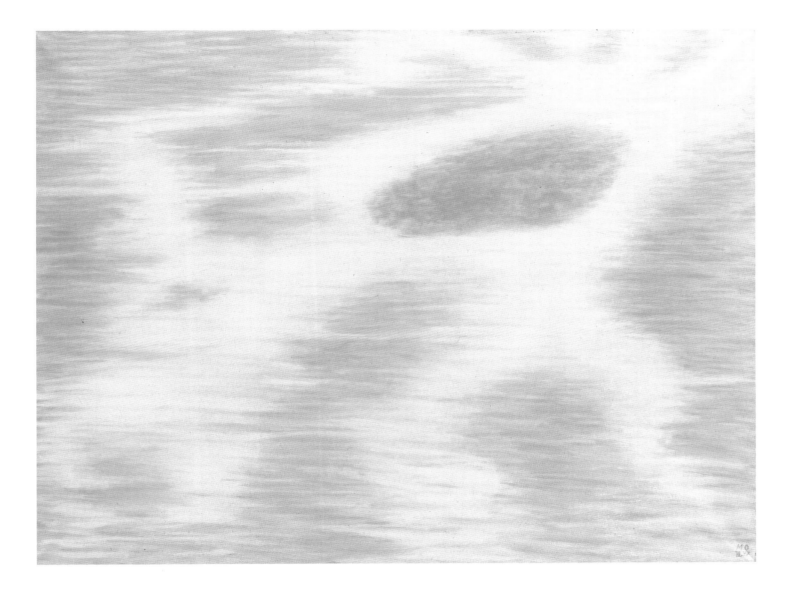

90

Meerlilie / Lily of the Sea, 1977. Oil on canvas, 44⅞ × 57½ in (114 × 146 cm). Galerie Renée Ziegler, Zurich

91

Unterirdische Schleife / Subterranean Bow, 1977. Bronze, 4⁵⁄₁₆ × 3⅜ × ⁷⁄₁₆ in
(12.5 × 8.5 × 1 cm). Galerie Renée Ziegler, Zurich

Dunkle Berge, rechts gelb-rote Wolken / Dark Mountains, Red and Yellow Clouds at Right, 1977–79. Oil on canvas, 25⁷⁄₁₆ × 31⁷⁄₈ in (64.5 × 81 cm). Aargauer Kunsthaus, Aarau, Switzerland

93

Neue Sterne / New Stars, 1977–82. Oil on canvas, 80¹¹⁄₁₆ × 98⁷⁄₁₆ in (205 × 250 cm). Kunstmuseum Bern

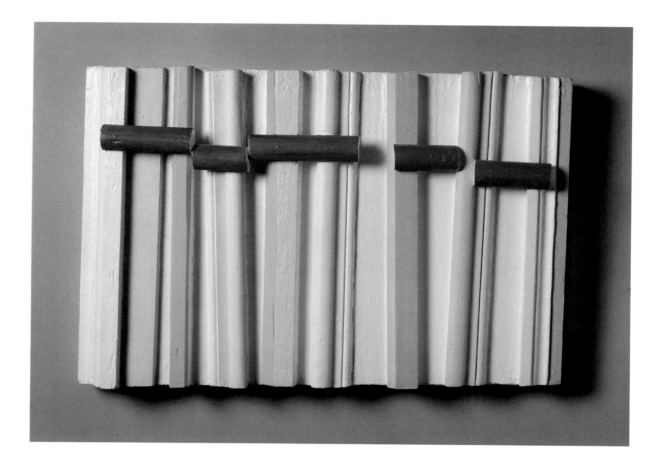

Vorhang / Curtain, 1978. Oil on wood, 18⁵⁄₁₆ × 26⁵⁄₈ in (46.5 × 67.5 cm). Galerie Renée Ziegler, Zurich

Weak, weaker, left.

The living to the left.

The dead ahead.

The stubborn will approach soon.

Who whistles once, does not belong here.

He will be sifted, respected

And nine and well slaughtered

And at last the hairs are empty.   1934

1980s

Ein Augenblick / A Moment, 1981. Oil on canvas, 9½ × 7½ in (24 × 19 cm). Private collection, Zurich

96

Ein angenehmer Moment auf einem Planeten / A Pleasant Moment on a Planet, 1981. Oil on canvas, 31⅞ × 39⅜ in (81 × 100 cm). Private collection

Für Bettine Brentano / For Bettine Brentano, 1983. Oil on canvas, 34¹³⁄₁₆ × 45¼ in (88.5 × 115 cm). Kunstmuseum Bern

98

Für Karoline von Günderode / For Karoline von Günderode, 1983. Oil on canvas, 38³⁄₁₆ × 51³⁄₁₆ in (97 × 130 cm). Kunstmuseum Bern

99

Stein, halb Kohle, halb Luft / Stone, Half Coal, Half Air, 1985. Gouache and pencil, 23¹⁄₁₆ × 18⅞ in (58.5 × 48 cm). Galerie Renée
Ziegler, Zurich

Zwei Geier, Rücken an Rücken / Two Vultures Back to Back, 1985. Gouache on black paper, 26⅜ × 20⅛ in (67 × 51 cm).
Collection Meret Schulthess-Bühler, Switzerland

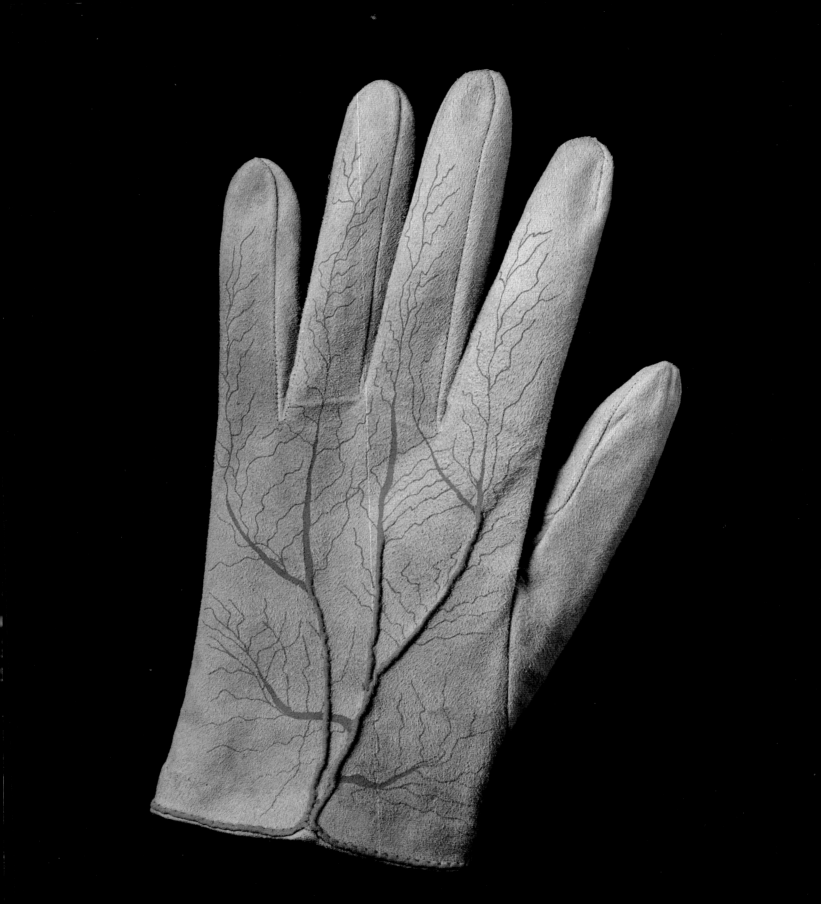

Handschuhe (Paar) / Pair of Gloves, 1985. Suede goatskin with piping and silkscreen; edition created for *Parkett* No. 4; each glove, $8^{11}/_{16} \times 3\frac{3}{8}$ in (22×8.5 cm).
Courtesy Parkett-Verlag, Zurich

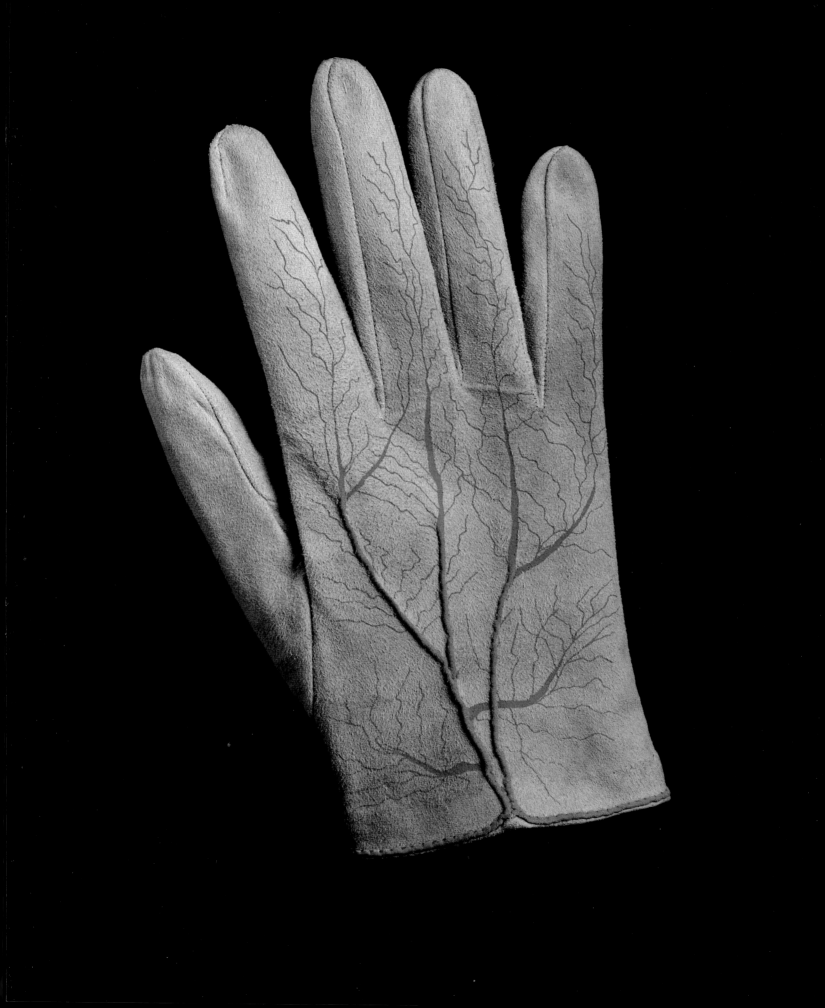

Meret Oppenheim was born in 1913 in Berlin. Her father was German, her mother, Swiss. During the First World War, she stayed with her grandparents in Switzerland. Her grandmother was a successful writer of children's books, which are still well known in Switzerland. After the war, the family moved to southern Germany and subsequently to Basel.

At fourteen, stimulated by her father's interest in Carl Gustav Jung, Oppenheim started recording her dreams, which was to become a lifelong habit and source of inspiration. In 1930, still a student, she drew the equation $X = Hare$ in her math notebook, which was reproduced in 1957 in the magazine *Le Surréalisme même 3* and titled *Le cahier d'une écolière (A Schoolgirl's Notebook)*. Instead of finishing high school, she decided to quit her formal studies and become an artist. In Basel, she met the painters Walter Kurt Wiemken and Irène Zurkinden. In Switzerland, at her grandparents' summer home in Carona, Ticino, she made the acquaintance of such people as Dadaist writer Hugo Ball, his wife, Emmy, and author Hermann Hesse, who was briefly married to her aunt Ruth Wenger.

When she was nineteen, Oppenheim moved to Paris, intending to study at the Académie de la Grande Chaumière, but she preferred to work on her own. She wrote poetry and made drawings, collages, and assemblages. In 1933, she was invited by Alberto Giacometti and Hans Arp to exhibit with the Surrealists in the *Salon des Surindépendants*. She also frequented the circle around André Breton at the Café de la Place Blanche.

Meret Oppenheim and Iréne Zurkinden in Paris in the Café du Dôme, 1932

In 1936, Alfred Barr Jr. acquired the object *Le déjeuner en fourrure* for The Museum of Modern Art, New York. The title, conceived by Breton, was inspired by Edouard Manet's painting *Déjeuner sur l'herbe* and Leopold Sacher-Masoch's novel *Venus im Pelz* (Venus in Fur). With her dry wit, Oppenheim always insisted that the "fur cup" was created by chance. She had been trying to make money in Paris by designing jewelry and clothes. One day, while sitting at the Café de Flore with Dora Maar and Pablo Picasso, they began talking about the fur-covered metal bracelet Oppenheim was wearing, which she had created for Elsa Schiapparelli. They toyed with the idea that anything could be covered with fur, whereupon Oppenheim remarked, "Why not this cup, saucer, and spoon?" When Breton invited her to contribute to an exhibition of Surrealist objects at the Galerie Charles Ratton, she went to a Parisian department store, bought a big cup with saucer and spoon, and covered all three with gazelle fur.

Meret Oppenhein and Leonor Fini at Galerie Gasser, Zurich, 1942

Her first solo show took place that same year at the Galerie Schulthess in Basel. Max Ernst wrote the invitation text. The object *Ma gouvernante—My Nurse—mein Kindermädchen,* on view at this exhibition, was acquired years later by the Moderna Museet in Stockholm.

Short of money, she decided to return to Basel in 1937. Because of his Jewish name, her physician father was unable to continue his practice in Germany and moved the family to Switzerland. Meret attended the School of Arts and Crafts for two years, earning some income restoring paintings and doing portraits. She became involved with "Group 33" and contributed to exhibitions organized by the Swiss Artists Association "Allianz." That year saw the beginning of a chronic depression that was to last eighteen years, during which time she continued to produce but frequently destroyed her work or left it unfinished.

In 1938, she traveled through northern Italy with artists Leonor Fini and André Pieyre de Mandiargues. In 1939, she submitted *Table with Bird's Feet* to an exhibition of fantasty furniture with works by Max Ernst, Fini, and others at the Galerie René Drouin et Leo Castelli in Paris.

The Kunstmuseum, Basel, purchased the painting *War and Peace* in 1943. Two years later, Oppenheim met Wolfgang La Roche, whom she married in 1949. They lived in and near Bern, where the Kunsthalle director Arnold Rüdlinger gradually introduced Oppenheim to the local art scene.

She returned to Paris in 1950 after more than a ten-year absence. On meeting some of her old friends from the thirties, she was disappointed because she felt that they had stagnated. Finally overcoming her prolonged crisis in 1954, two years later Oppenheim designed costumes and masks for Daniel Spoerri's production in Bern of Picasso's *How to Catch Wishes by the Tail*. For her exhibition on view at the same time, she created the object *The Couple*.

In 1959, Meret Oppenheim created a spring banquet presented on the body of a nude woman in which a coterie of close friends—three couples, including the woman on the table—participated. Breton urged her to reenact the scene a few months later for the Exposition InteRnatiOnale de Surréalisme (EROS) at the Galerie Cordier in Paris, the last joint exhibition of the Surrealists. She chose not to do so, but allowed Breton to recreate the piece. Later, she regretted this decision because Breton's reenactment became a public rather than a private event, changing her original intention.

Gradually, starting in the late sixties, there was a revival of interest in Oppenheim's work with solo and group exhibitions in Basel, Paris, Milan, New York, Zurich, Bern, Stockholm, Oslo, and Geneva. In 1967, Pontus Hulten and Carl Frederick Reuterswärd organized a retrospective at the Moderna Museet in Stockholm. In December of that year, her husband died. She moved to Bern and in 1972, rented a second studio in Paris. The 1974–75 retrospective that toured Solothurn and Winterthur, Switzerland, and Duisburg, Germany, clearly revealed Oppenheim's affinity with the work of younger artists in Europe at that

Meret Oppenheim modeling for a magazine fashion shoot, circa 1945 (Photo: Hans Richter)

Meret Oppenheim and friends in a club in Murten, Switzerland, 1961 (left to right: Peter Petulius, Meret Oppenheim, Vincent Carter, Lilly Keller, and Annemarie Kuriger) (Photo: Toni Grieb)

time. On January 16, 1975, she was presented with the Art Award of the City of Basel. Her acceptance speech in which she commented that "every person is both male and female" and that women are the "muses whom genius has kissed," attracted considerable attention.

Although she had always written poetry, it was not until 1981 that her first collection of poems (1933–57), *Sansibar*, was published with silk-screen prints, by Edition Fanal, Basel. In 1982, she was awarded the Art Prize of the City of Berlin and also invited to take part in *documenta 7* in Kassel. A year later, the Goethe Institute organized a retrospective that was shown in Genoa, Milan, and Naples, and included two important new paintings, *For Bettine Brentano* and *For Karoline von Günderode*. These paintings were inspired by the published correspondence between the two Romantic writers from 1802 to 1806, which Oppenheim called "Hymnic Conversations." Also in 1983, her fountain sculpture at the Waisenhausplatz in Bern was unveiled and met with controversial press reaction. In 1984, she again enjoyed a retrospective exhibition at the Bern Kunsthalle and the ARC-Musée d'Art Moderne de la Ville de Paris. The German publishing house Suhrkamp in Frankfurt am Main released another collection of her poems. In 1985, she finalized the design for her fountain sculpture in the Jardin de l'Ancienne Ecole Polytechnique in Paris.

Meret Oppenheim died in Basel on November 15, 1985, the day her book *Caroline* was released to the public.

Jacqueline Burckhardt and Bice Curiger

Meret Oppenheim in the early 1980s (Photo: Nanda Lanfranco)

Selected Exhibitions

Solo Exhibitions

1936   Galerie Schulthess, Basel
1952   Galerie d'Art Moderne, Basel
1956   A l'Étoile Scellée, Paris
1957   Galerie Riehentor, Basel
1959   Galerie Riehentor, Basel
1960   Galleria Arturo Schwarz, Milan
        Casa Serodine, Ascona, Switzerland
1965   Galerie Gimpel und Hanover, Zurich
1967   Retrospective, Moderna Museet, Stockholm
1968   Galerie Krebs, Bern
1969   Galerie der Spiegel, Cologne
        Galleria La Medusa, Rome
        Editions Claude Givaudan, Paris
1970   Galleria Il Fauno, Turin
1971   *Caché-Trouvé*, Galerie Bonnier, Geneva
1972   Wilhelm-Lehmbruck-Museum, Duisburg, Germany
        Galerie d'Art Moderne, Basel
1973   *Solitudes mariées*, Galerie S. Visat, Paris
1974   Galerie Renée Ziegler, Zurich
        Galerie Ziegler S.A., Geneva
        Galerie Müller, Stuttgart
        Jeux d'été, Galerie Arman Zerbib, Paris
1974–75 Museum der Stadt, Solothurn, Switzerland;
        Kunstmuseum, Winterthur, Switzerland;
        Wilhelm-Lehmbruck-Museum, Duisberg, Germany
1975   Galleria San Lucca, Bologna
        Galerie 57, Biel, Switzerland
1977   Galerie Elisabeth Kaufmann, Basel
        Galerie Loeb, Bern
        Galerie Nothelfer, Berlin
        Galerie Gerhild Grolitsch, Munich
        Galerie Boulakia, Paris
1978   Eugenia Cucalon Gallery, New York
        Galerie Levy, Hamburg
1979   Kunstverein, Wolfsburg, Germany
1980   Galerie 57, Biel, Switzerland
        Marian Goodman Gallery, New York
1981   Galerie Edition Claude Givaudan, Geneva
        Galerie Nächst St. Stephan, Vienna
1982   Galerie Krinzinger, Innsbruck, Austria
        Kärntener Landesgalerie, Klagenfurt, Austria
        Salzburger Kunstverein, Salzburg
        Galleria Pieroni, Rome

Meret Oppenheim at the Moderna Museet, Stockholm, on the occasion of her retrospective, 1967

        Akademie der Künste, Berlin
        Kunsthalle, Bern
1983   Touring exhibition organized by Goethe Institute. Traveled to Genoa, Milan, Naples, and Turin.
1984   Nantenshi Gallery, Tokyo
        Kunsthalle, Bern
        ARC-Musée d'Art Moderne de la Ville de Paris
1985   Galerie Susan Wyss, Zurich
        Galerie Oestermalen, Stockholm
        Galerie Beatrix Wilhelm, Stuttgart
        Kunstverein, Frankfurt
        Haus am Waldsee, Berlin
        Kunstverein, Munich
        Galerie Stemmle-Adler, Heidelberg
        Atelier Fanal, Basel
1986   Kunsthalle, Winterthur, Switzerland
        Galleria Gamarra y Garrigues, Madrid
1987   Galerie Krebs, Bern
        Kunstmuseum Bern
        Galerie Renée Ziegler, Zurich
1988   Kent Gallery, New York
1989   ICA, London
        Bilderstreit, Cologne
        Rooseum, Malmö, Sweden
        M.O., Galerie des Bastions, Geneva
        M.O., Galerie Pudelko, Bonn
1990   Palau de la Virreina, ICA, Barcelona
1991   *M.O. Masken*, Freitagsgalerie Imhof, Solothurn, Switzerland
        Un moment agréable sur une planète, Centre Culturel Suisse, Paris
1993   *Hommage à Meret Oppenheim*, Galerie Schön + Halepa, Berlin
1994   *Meret Oppenheim*, Aktionsforum Praterinsel, Munich
1995   Museo d'arte, Mendrisio, Switzerland
        Kunstverein, Ulm, Germany
        Galerie A. von Scholz, Berlin

Group Exhibitions

Weihnachtsausstellung bernischer Maler und Bildhauer,
   Kunsthalle, Bern, and Helmhaus, Zurich
Sammlung Marguerite Arp-Hagenbach, Kunstmuseum, Basel
Weihnachtsausstellung, Thunerhof, Thun, Switzerland
1968 *Horizonte 2*, Galerie Gimpel und Hanover, Zurich
Salon de Mai, Musée d'Art Moderne, Paris
The Obsessive Image 1960–1968, Carlton House
   Terrace, London
Dada, Surrealism and Their Heritage, The Museum of
   Modern Art, New York
Berner Galerie, Bern
Trésors du Surréalisme, Casino, Knokke, Belgium
1969 *Salon de Mai*, Musée d'Art Moderne, Paris
Napoléon 1969, Landesmuseum, Schleswig, Germany
Vier Freunde, Kunsthalle, Bern–Dusseldorf
Surrealismus in Europa, Baukunst-Galerie, Cologne
650 Minis, Galerie Krebs, Bern
Weihnachtsausstellung, Kunsthalle, Basel
1970 *5 Schweizerische Plastikausstellung*, Biel, Switzerland
160 x 160 x 38, Berner Galerie, Bern
Surrealism, Moderna Museet, Stockholm; Konsthall Göteborg,
   Museum, Sundsvall, Museum, Malmö, Sweden;
   Kunsthalle, Nuremberg
Das Ding als Objekt, Museum, Oslo
1971 *11 Schweizer*, Galerie Vontobel, Feldmeilen
Salon de Mai, Musée d'Art Moderne, Paris
Métamorphoses de l'objet, Palais des Beaux-Arts,
   Brussels; Rotterdam–Berlin–Milan
Multiples, Kunstgewerbeschule, Basel
Sturmkonstnärer och Schweizisk Nukonst, Museum,
   Landskrona, Sweden
Ich mich, Berner Galerie, Bern
Baukunst, Der Geist des Surrealismus, Cologne
9 Schweizer Künstler, Galerie S-Press, Hattingen-
   Blankenstein, Germany
Galerie Alphonse Chave, Vence, France
Alfred Hofkunst, Meret Oppenheim, Peter von Wattenwyl,
   Galerie Krebs, Bern
1972 *Art Suisse contemporain*, Bochum, Germany–Tel Aviv
Artistes Suisses contemporains, Grand Palais, Paris
Le Surréalisme 1922–1942, Musée des Arts Décoratifs, Paris
Die andere Realität, Kunstmuseum Bern
Berner Galerie, Bern
Schweizer Zeichnungen im 20. Jahrhundert, Staatliche Graphische
   Sammlung, Munich; Kunstmuseum, Winterthur;
   Kunstmuseum, Bern; Musée Rath, Geneva
Der Surréalismus, Haus der Kunst, Munich and
   Musée des Arts Décoratifs, Paris

Meret Oppenheim at Gallery Levy, 1978

Gchribelet + Gchritzlet, Galerie 57, Biel, Switzerland
La table de Diane, Galerie Christofle, Paris
31 artistes Suisses, Grand Palais, Paris
Salon de Mai, Paris
Profile X, Schweizer Kunst Heute, Museum, Bochum, Germany
L'estampe et le surréalisme, Galerie Vision Nouvelle, Paris
1973 Galerie Krebs, Bern
Art Boxes, Kunsthandel Brinkman, Amsterdam
Les Masques, Galerie Germain, Paris
Tell 73, Zurich–Basel–Lugano–Bern–Lausanne
Weisser Saal, Bern
Galerie Fred Lanzenberg, Brussels
Moderne Schweizer Künstler, Warsaw
Katakombe, Idole, Basel
1974 *Micro-Salon*, Galerie Christofle, Paris
Lapopie, Galerie Françoise Tournier, Château de
   Saint-Cirq, France
Aspects du Surréalisme, Galerie Françoise Tournier, Paris
Moderne Schweizer Künstler, Budapest-Bucharest
Accrochage, Galerie Luise Krohn, Badenweiler, Germany
Salon de Mai, Paris
1975 *Magna—Feminismus und Kreativität*, Galerie
   Nächst St. Stephan, Vienna
Machines Célibataires, Edition 999, Düsseldorf;
   Bern–Venice–Brussels–Le Creusot–Paris–Malmö–
   Amsterdam–Vienna
Siège—Poème, Paris–Créteil–Montreal, Quebec;
   Weisser Saal, Bern
Aspekte aus neuen Solothurner Sammlungen, Museum der Stadt,
   Solothurn, Switzerland

Selected Bibliography

Almanach neuer Kunst in der Schweiz. ed. "Allianz," Zurich, in collaboration with the Moderner Schweizer Künstler, 1939.

Ammann, Jean-Christophe. "Liebe Meret." In *Basler Zeitung*, Basel, November 16, 1985.

Amodei-Mebel, A. "Meret Oppenheim," thesis for Professor Rossetti, Academy of Fine Arts, Rome, 1984–85.

André Breton, Paul Éluard, Man Ray: Meret Oppenheim. Editions des Cahiers d'Art, 2nd ed., Paris, 1934.

Arici, Laura. "Der Hermaphroditische Engel. 'Imago'—einen Film über Meret Oppenheim." In *Neue Zürcher Zeitung*, Zurich, December 16, 1988.

Auffermann, Verena. "Neue Kleider für neue Ideen." In *Frankfurter Rundschau*, Frankfurt, January 3, 1985.

"Auflehnung ziemt sich für Frauen." In *Basler Zeitung*, Basel, January 18, 1975.

Auregli, Dede. "Oppenheim, il sogno delle cose." In *L'Unità*, Italy, November 21, 1985.

Barletta, Riccardo. "Oppenheim: Più fine di Duchamp." In *Corriere della sera*, Italy, October 12, 1983.

Barr Jr., Alfred H. *Fantastic Art Dada Surrealism*. New York: The Museum of Modern Art, 1936.

Baumer, Dorothea. "Poetisches von einer Rebellin." In *Süddeutsche Zeitung*, Germany, July 1, 1985.

Baumgartner, Marcel. *L'Art pour l'Aare. Bernische Kunst im 20. Jahrhundert*, Bern, 1984.

Bezzola, Leonardo. "Objekte von Meret Oppenheim. Photoreportage." In *Werk* No. 4, Zurich, 1971.

Billeter, Erika. "Eine Säge wird Vogel." In *Züri Leu*, Zurich, November 23, 1973.

Billeter, Fritz. "Wie leicht, wie schwer fiel ihr dies Leben." In *Tages-Anzeiger*, Zurich, November 16, 1985.

Boone, Danièle. "Meret Oppenheim" (Entretien). In *L'Humidité*, Paris, 1976.

Borrini, Catherine France. "Les folies Oppenheim." In *L'Hebdo*, Paris, September 13, 1984.

Breton, André. "Magie quotidienne." In *La tour Saint-Jacques*, Paris, November/December 1955.

Burckhardt, Jacqueline. "The Semantics of Antics." In *Parkett* No. 4, Zurich, 1985.

Burri, Peter. "Freiheit wird nicht gegeben, man muss sie nehmen." In *Die Weltwoche* No. 47, Germany, November 21, 1985.

Butler, Sheila. *Psychoanalysis, Ageny and Androgyny*, M.A. thesis, University of Western Ontario, London, Ontario, 1993.

Calas, Nicolas. "Meret Oppenheim: Confrontations." In *Artforum*, New York, Summer 1978.

Calzolari, Ginestra. "Se 'Man Ray dipinge per essere amato' Meret Oppenheim dipinge per amare e essere amata." In *Acrobat Mime Parfait* No. 1, Bologna, 1981.

Cameron, Dan. *What Is Contemporary Art?* Exhibition catalogue. Rooseum, Malmö, Sweden, 1989.

Catoir, Barbara. "Der Geruch, Das Geräusch, Die Zeit. Zu den Gedichten von Meret Oppenheim." In *Akzente. Zeitschrift für Literatur*, Heft 1, Munich, 1975.

Chadwick, Whitney. *Women Artists and the Surrealist Movement*. Boston: Little, Brown, and Co., 1963.

Christ, Dorothea. "Die Übergabe des Baselr Kunstpreises an Meret Oppenheim." In *Kunst-Bulletin, Berne*, February 1975.

Corà, Bruno. "M.O.: quando l'artista è musa di se stessa." In *Napoli Oggi*, Naples, April 12, 1984.

Curiger, Bice. "Una storia cominciata con alcune foto di Man Ray e una colazione in pelliccia." In *Bolaffiarte* No. 103, Turin, 1980.

———. "Ein Werk voller Offenbarungen und Geheimnisse." In *Tages-Anzeiger*, Zurich, March 18, 1982.

———. *Meret Oppenheim, Spuren durchstandener Freiheit*. With Catalogue Raisonné by Meret Oppenheim and Dominque Bürgi, Zurich: ABC Publishers, 1982.

———. "Meret Oppenheim: Ich bin noch kein Denkmal!" In *Tages-Anzeiger (Züri-Tip)*, Zurich, September 16, 1983.

———. "Abschied von Meret Oppenheim." In *Emma* No. 1, 1986.

———. *Meret Oppenheim: Defiance in the Face of Freedom*. With Catalogue Raisonné by Meret Oppenheim and Dominique Bürgi. Zurich: Parkett Publishers, and Cambridge, MA: The MIT Press, 1989.

———. *Meret Oppenheim: Tracce di una libertà sofferta*. Lugano: Fidia edizioni d'arte, Lugano, 1995.

———, Rita Bischof, Johannes Gachnang, Christoph Bürgi. *Ansprachen anlässlich der Abdankung von Meret Oppenheim*, edited by Burkhard Wenger, private publication, Switzerland, 1985.

D'Amico, Fabrizio. "Brillano le lacrime di Meret." In *La Repubblica*, Rome, February 28, 1982.

———. "Quando una tazza indossa la pelliccia." In *La Repubblica*, Rome, October 14, 1983.

De Feugas, Jean-Claude. "Conversation avec Meret Oppenheim." In *Créatis* No. 5, Paris, 1977.

Dictionnaire abrégé du surréalisme. Ed. Galerie Beaux-Arts, Paris, 1938.

Ditzen, Lore. "Die Dame mit der Pelztasse." In *Süddeutsche Zeitung*, Munich, March 27/28, 1982.

documenta 7/Kassel. Exhibition catalogue,1982. Einladungskarte.
 Max Ernst: Meret Oppenheim. Galerie Marguerite Schulthess,
 Basel, 1936.

Florence, Penny and Dee Reynolds. *Feminist Subjects Multi Media.*
 Manchester University Press, 1995.

*Frammenti Interfacce Intervalli, Paradigmi della Frammentazione nell'Arte
 svizzera*, Catalogo della Mostra. a cura di Viana Conti, Edizioni
 Costa & Nolan, Genova, 1992.

Frey, Patrick. "Die Antilope mit Sonne auf dem Rücken." In *Die
 Wochenzeitung* No. 36, Zurich, September 7, 1984.

Gachnang, Johannes. "A Meret." *Meret Oppenheim. Disegni*. Invitation
 from Galleria Pieroni, Rome, December 1981.

Gallery Levy. "Meret Oppenheim. Zwei–vier–sechs–acht and forever."
 Schwetzingen: K. F. Schimper-Verlag, 1987.

Gauville, Hervé. "Meret Oppenheim meurt en Suisse." In *Libération*,
 Paris, November 18, 1985.

Gensicke, A. "Meret Oppenheim, The Surrealistic Artist," seminar
 paper for Professor U.M. Schneede, Munich, 1986.

Gibson, Michael. "The Fantasy and Wit of Meret Oppenheim." In
 International Herald Tribune, Paris, November 24/25, 1984.

Glozer, Laszlo. "Schöne Respektlosigkeit." In *Süddeutsche Zeitung*,
 Munich, October 19, 1977.

Grosskopf, Annegret. "Die eigenwillige Lady." In *Stern*, November 25,
 1982.

Grut, Mario. "Madame! Har ni nonsin durckitur den här pälsen?" In
 Vecko Journalen, Stockholm, April 28, 1967.

Häsli, Richard. "Fährtenleserin des Unbewussten. Meret Oppenheim
 zum 70. Geburtstag." In *Neue Zürcher Zeitung*, Zurich, October
 6, 1983.

———. "Auf den Spuren des Unbewussten." In *Neue Zürcher Zeitung*,
 Zurich, November 16/17, 1985.

Hecht, Axel. "Ideenblitze vom poetischen Irrlicht." In *art, Das
 Kunstmagazin*, Hamburg, June 1982.

Helfenstein, Josef. *Meret Oppenheim und Surrealismus*. Dissertation.
 University, Bern, 1991.

———. *Meret Oppenheim und der Surrealismus*, Stuttgart: Verlag
 G. Hatje, 1993.

Helvetische Steckbriefe. Exhibition catalogue. Researched by the Zurich
 Seminar für Literaturkritik with Werner Weber (Christina
 Baumann). Helmhaus, Zurich. Zurich and Munich: Artemis
 Publishers, 1981.

Henry, Maurice. "Meret Oppenheim." In *Antologia grafica del
 Surrealismo*, Album 3, Milan, 1972.

Henry, Ruth. "Traüme vom Kosmos." In *Publik*, Cologne, February
 14, 1969.

———. "Sogno sul Cosmo di Meret, Träume vom Kosmos." In
 Quinta. Exhibition catalogue. Contributions by Max Ernst,
 Frederick Reuterswärd and Benjamin Péret. Stockholm:
 Moderna Museet, 1967.

———. "Interview mit Meret Oppenheim, zum 70. Geburtstag." In
 Du, October 1983.

Hofmann, Werner. *Laudatio auf Meret Oppenheim*. Grosser Kunstpreis
 der Stadt Berlin. Akademie der Künste, Berlin, 1982.

Hollenstein, Roman. "Auf der Suche nach dem Ideal der Kunst." In
 Neue Zürcher Zeitung No. 210, Zurich, September 10, 1984.

Huber, Jörg. "Man muss sich die Freiheit nehmen." In *Der schweizerische Beobachter* No. 12,1987.

Indiana, Gary. "A Curious Part of the Planet." In *The Village Voice*,
 New York, March 29, 1988.

Isler, Ursula. "Meret Oppenheim." In *Neue Zürcher Zeitung*, Zurich,
 December 4, 1973.

———. "Mit der Kraft der Stille." In *Neue Zürcher Zeitung*, Zurich,
 March 27, 1982.

Jouffroy, Alain. "Meret Oppenheim." In *Opus International* nos. 19/20,
 Paris, October 1970.

———. *A l'improviste*. Invitation from Galerie Suzanne Visat, Paris,
 February 1973.

Keller, Renate. "Sehr geehrte Meret Oppenheim." In *55. Jahresbericht
 des Kunstvereins Winterthur*, Winterthur, Switzerland, 1975.

Kipphoff, Petra. "Kunst ist Interpretation. ZEIT-Gespräch mit Meret
 Oppenheim." In *Die Zeit* No. 47, Hamburg, November 19,
 1982.

———. "Zauberin in den Lagunen." In *Die Zeit*, November 22, 1985.

Klüver, A., Martin, J. *Kiki's Paris*. New York: Harry N. Abrams, Inc.,
 1989.

Legacy to the Kunstmuseum Bern. Exhibition catalogue. Hans-Christoph
 von Tavel: "Das Vermächtnis von Meret Oppenheim im
 Kunstmuseum." Josef Helfenstein: "Androgynität als
 Bildthema und Persönlichkeitsmodell." Christiane Meyer-
 Thoss: "Protokoll der Gespräche mit Meret Oppenheim."
 Isabel Schulz: "Qui êtes-vous? Who are you? Wer sind Sie?",
 Bern, 1987.

Levy, Thomas. *Meret Oppenheim, zwei–vier–sechs and forever*.
 Schwetzingen: K. F. Schimper Verlag, 1988.

Lüscher, Helen. "Meret Oppenheim." In *Kunst-Nachrichten, Zeitschrift
 für internationale Kunst*, Heft 5, Lucerne, February 1970.

Matthews, Harry. "Meret Oppenheim." *The Paris Review*, No. 36,
 Paris, 1950.

Mendini, Alessandro. "Cara Meret Oppenheim." In *Domus* No. 605,
 Milan, 1980.

Meret Oppenheim. Exhibition catalogue. Foreword: André Kamber,
 Rudolf Koella, Siegfried Salzmann. With contributions by
 André Pieyre de Mandiargues, Benjamin Péret, Helmut
 Heissenbüttel, Alain Jouffroy, Hans Christoph von Tavel.
 Museum der Stadt, Solothurn, 1974.

Meret Oppenheim. Exhibition catalogue. Galerie nächst St. Stephan, Vienna; Galerie Krinziger, Innsbruck; Kärntener Landesgalerie, Klagenfurt; Salzburger Kunstverein, Salzburg, 1981.

Meret Oppenheim in conversation with Henry-Alexis Baatsch. Exhibition catalogue. Galerie de Séoul, Seoul, 1982.

Meret Oppenheim. Exhibition catalogue. Palazzo Bianco, Genoa; Padiglione d'Arte Contemporanea, Milan; Museo Diego Aragona Pignatelli, Naples; Galleria Martano, Turin. With contributions by Ida Gianelli, Bernhard Wittek, Meret Oppenheim, Johannes Gachnang, Bice Curiger, 1983

Meret Oppenheim. Exhibition catalogue. Foreword by Jürgen Glaesemer. Galerie Levy, Hamburg, 1978.

Meret Oppenheim. Exhibition catalogue. Essay by Jean-Hubert Martin and Jim Palette, Kunsthalle, Bern, 1984.

Meret Oppenheim. Exhibition catalogue. ARC-Musée d'Art Moderne de la Ville de Paris, 1984.

Meret Oppenheim. Exhibition Catalogue. Kent Gallery, New York, 1988.

"Meret Oppenheim." Zur Ausstellung im Aktionsforum Praterinsel, Munich, 1994.

Meyer-Thoss, Christiane. "Poetry at Work." In *Parkett* No. 4, Zurich, 1985.

————. *Bilderstreit*. Exhibition catalogue. Museum Ludwig in den Rheinhallen der Kölner Messe, Cologne, 1989.

————. *Meret Oppenheim "Buch der Ideen."* Bern-Berlin: Gachnang & Springer, 1995.

Monteil, Annemarie. "Die alte Schlange Natur." In *Weltwoche*, October 9, 1974.

————. "Meret Oppenheim." In *Kunst und Frau*, Club Hrotsvit, Sonderheft, Schweizerischer Verein für Kulturelle Tätigkeit, Lucerne, 1975.

————. "Meret Oppenheim: Die Idee mit dem Brunnen." In *du*, Zurich, October 1980.

————. "Wirf alle Steine hinter dich und lass die Wände los." In *Basler Zeitung*, November 16, 1985.

————. "Die Weisheit aus dem Felsenverlies." In *Künstler, Kritisches Lexikon der Gegenwartskunst*. Munich: Weltkunst und Bruckmann Verlag, 1988.

Neue Sachlichkeit und Surrealismus in der Schweiz 1915–1940. Exhibition catalogue. Kunstmuseum Winterthur. Bern: Benteli-Verlag, 1979.

Parete, documenti del Surrealismo I, Turin, April 1971.

Picon, Gaëtan. *Der Surrealismus in Wort und Bild*. Geneva: Verlag Skira, 1976.

Prerost, Irene. "Eine junge alte Dame." In *Schweizer Illustrierte Zeitung*, September 3, 1984.

Rotzler, Willy. *Objekt-Kunst, von Duchamp bis Kienholz*. Cologne: Verlag DuMont-Schauberg, 1972.

Salerno, Giovan Battista. "Una tazzina di caffè in pelliccia dall'incantevole Meret Oppenheim." In *Manifesto*, Rome, February 2, 1982.

Schierle, Barbara. "Die Freiheit muss man nehmen." In *Tip* No. 8, Berlin, April, 1982.

Schlocker, Georges. "Sie ist doch längst über die Pelztasse hinaus." In *Saarbrücker Zeitung*, Saarbrücken, March 18, 1982.

Schloss, Edith. "Galeries in Rome." In *International Herald Tribune*, Paris, January 16/17, 1982.

Schmid, Doris. "Auf anderen Sternen weiterleben." In *Süddeutsche Zeitung*, November 18, 1985.

Schneede, Uwe M. Malerei des Surrealismus. Cologne: Verlag M. DuMont-Schauberg, 1973.

Schulz, Isabel. *Meret Oppenheim*, Dissertation. University of Hamburg, 1993.

Schumann, Sarah. "Fragen und Assoziationen zu den Arbeiten von Meret Oppenheim." Exhibition catalogue. In *Künstlerinnen international*, Schloss Charlottenburg, Berlin, 1977.

Sello, Gottfried. "Meret Oppenheim." In *Brigitte* No. 4, Hamburg, 1980.

Smith, Roberta. "Meret Oppenheim." In *The New York Times*, March 18, 1988.

Strobl, Ingrid. "Meret Oppenheim: Die Schöne und das Biest." In *Emma, Zeitschrift für Frauen von Frauen*, Berlin, July 1981.

Tatort Bern. Exhibition catalogue. Museum Bochum, Kunstsammlung. Bern: Zytglogge-Verlag, 1976.

Thorson, Victoria. *Great Drawings of the 20th Century*. New York: Sharewood, 1982.

Tillman, Lynne. "Don't Cry-Work. Interview with Meret Oppenheim." In *Art and Artists*, London, October 1973.

"Un moment agréable sur une planète." Exhibition catalogue. Centre Culturel Suisse, Paris, 1991.

Vachtova, Ludmila. "Ohne mich ohnehin ohne Weg kam ich dahin." In *Tages-Anzeiger*, Zurich, September 14, 1984.

Vergine, Lea. *L'altra metà dell'avanguardia 1910–1940*. Exhibition catalogue. Palazzo Reale di Milano; Palazzo delle Esposizioni, Rome; Kulturhuset, Stockholm, 1980.

————. "Der Weg zur anderen Hälfte der Avantgarde." In *Transatlantik*, Munich, March 1981.

von Helmolt, Christa. "Die Zeit ist ihr treue Verbündete." In *Frankfurter Allgemeine Zeitung*, Frankfurt, January 3, 1985.

von Moos-Kaminski, Gisela. "Meret Oppenheim." In *Artefactum*, February-March 1985.

von Tavel, Hans-Christoph. "Meret Oppenheim und ihre Biographie." In *Berner Kunstmitteilungen*, Bern, June/July 1987.

Waldberg, Patrick. *Meret Oppenheim et ses jeux d'été*. Exhibition catalogue. Galerie Armand Zerbib, Paris, 1974.

Walser, Paul L. "Frisches Lüftchen im Römer Kunstleben." In *Tages-Anzeiger*, Zurich, December 31, 1981.

Wehrli, Peter. "Worte in giftige Buchstaben eingepackt . . . (wird durchsichtig)." In *Orte, Schweizer Literaturzeitschrift*, Zurich, 1980.

Winter, Peter. "Kein mit weissem Marmor belegtes Brötchen." In *du*, Zurich, November 1978.

Withers, Josephine. "The Famous Fur-lined Teacup and the Anonymous Meret Oppenheim." In *Arts Magazine*, New York, November 1977.

Zacharopoulos, Denys. "Meret Oppenheim." In *Acrobat Mime Parfait* No. 1, Bologna, 1981.

Zaugg, Fred. "Zum Tode von Meret Oppenheim - am Ziel des Menschseins." In *Der Bund*, Bern, November 16, 1985.

Zimmermann, Marie-Louise. "Grosse Ehre für eine grosse Künstlerin." In *Der Bund*, Bern, February 4, 1982.

———. "Die Freiheit nehmen." In *Brückenbauer*, Zurich, February 19, 1982.

———. "Sie war mehr als nur eine grosse Surrealistin." In *Berner Zeitung*, November 16, 1985.

1954–55 Poetry and illustrations for Carl Laszlo's *La lune en rodage*, Basel.

1957 "Enquêtes." *Le Surréalisme même 3*, Autumn, Paris.

1959 "le Striptease, enquête." In *Le Surréalisme même 5*, Spring, Paris.

1967 "Objects and Poems." In *Icteric* No. 2.

1969 *Meret Oppenheim spricht Meret Oppenheim, man könnte sagen, etwas stimme nicht. Gedichte 1933 bis 1969.* S-Press-Tonband No. 19, Hattingen, Germany.

1975 Transcript of a speech given in Basel, January 16, 1975, on receiving the Art Award of the City of Basel. In *Kunst-Bulletin, Berne*, February.

1978 "Es gibt keine 'weibliche Kunst." In *Brückenbauer*, January 27, Zurich.

Belege, Gedichte aus der deutschsprachigen Schweiz seit 190. Werner Weber. Zurich and Munich: Artemis-Verlag.

1980 "Noch schwieriger ist es ein weiblicher Künstler zu sein." In *Orte, Schweizer Literaturzeitschrift*, July/August, Zurich.

"Io Meret." In *Bolaffiarte* No. 103, Turin.

1981 *Sansibar. Gedichte und Serigraphien von Meret Oppenheim.* Basel: Edition Fanal.

1982 "Weibliche Kunst." In *Tages-zeitung*, March 19, Berlin.

With Lys Wiedmer-Zingg. "Mir Fraue," *Schweizer Frauenblatt*, March, Erlenbach.

1983 "Soleil, Der Weisse Schein des Lichts, Demi- lune. A Project by Meret Oppenheim," In *Artforum*, October, New York.

1984 *Husch, Husch, der schönste Vokal entleert sich. Gedichte, Zeichnungen.*, ed. by Christiane Meyer-Thoss (postscript). Frankfurt am Main: Suhrkamp Verlag.

"Das Ende kann auch der Anfang sein," *Kunst und Wissenschaft*, ed. Paul Feyer-abend, vdf. Zurich: Verlag der Fachvereine.

1985 *Caroline. Gedichte und Radierungen von Meret Oppenheim.* Basel: Edition Fanal.

Text, drawings, and gloves. *Parkett* No. 4, Zurich.

1986 *Aufzeichnungen, 1928–85, Träume*, ed. by Christiane Meyer-Thoss. Bern/Berlin: Verlag Gachnang und Springer,

1987 *Kaspar Hauser oder Die Goldene Freiheit. Textvorlage für ein Drehbuch.* Bern/Berlin: Verlag Gachnang und Springer.

1996 *Quick, Quick, the Most Beautiful Vowel Is Voiding.* Los Angeles: Sun & Moon Press.

Filmography

1978   Christina von Braun (director). *Früstück im Pelz*. TV film, 45 mins., Norddeutscher Rundfunk (production agency), Germany.

1983   *Vis-à-vis: Meret Oppenheim im gespraech mit Franck A. Mayer*. TV film, 60 mins., DRS, Germany.

Jana Markovà (director). *Zu Besuch bei Meret Oppenheim in Paris*. TV film, 50 mins., Telefilm Saar (production agency), Germany.

1984   J. Canobbi, D. Bürgi (directors). *Einige Blicke auf Meret Oppenheim*. Video, 60 mins., Westdeutscher Rundfunk (production agency), Germany.

L. Thorn (director). *Porträt der Künstlerin Meret Oppenheim*. Video, 60 mins., RTL, November, ARC—Musée d'Art Moderne de la Ville de Paris.

Deidi von Schaewen, Heinz Schwerfel (directors). *Man Ray*. Video, 52 mins. Centre Georges Pompidou, Paris.

1985   Susanne Offenbach (director). *Zum Tod von Meret Oppenheim, mit Interview*. TV film, 15 mins., SW 3 (production agency), Germany.

1988   Pamela Robertson-Pearce, Anselm Spoerri (directors and producers). *Imago, Meret Oppenheim*. Film, 90 mins., England.

Meret Oppenheim at Bélvèdere, Carona, Switzerland, August 1985 from the film *Imago*. (Photo: Pamela Robertson-Pearce and Anselm Spoerri)

*Lenders to the Exhibition*

Aargauer Kunsthaus, Aarau
David Bowie
Adrian Bühler
Dominique Bürgi
Centre Georges Pompidou, Musée national d'art moderne
Collection Matta
Collection Onnasch, Berlin
Eugenia Cucalon Gallery, New York
Fondazione Marguerite Arp, Locarno
Fundación Yannick y Ben Jakober, Mallorca
Galerie Hauser & Wirth AG, Zurich
Galerie Renée Ziegler, Zurich
Foster and Monique Goldstrom
Marian Goodman Gallery, New York
Petra Kipphoff
Kunsthaus, Zurich
Kunstmuseum Bern
Kunstmuseum Olten
Kunstmuseum Solothurn
L.A.C., Switzerland
The Menil Collection, Houston
The Museum of Modern Art, New York
Museum moderner Kunst Stiftung Ludwig, Vienna
Öffentliche Kunstsammlung Basel, Kunstmuseum
Parkett-Verlag, Zurich
Private collections
Jacques and Marion Richter
San Francisco Museum of Modern Art
Meret Schulthess-Bühler
Amada Segarra
Swiss Bank Corporation Collection, Basel
Swiss Mobiliar Insurance Company, Bern
Swiss Reinsurance Company, Zurich
Ulmer Museum, Ulm, Germany
Birgit and Burkhard Wenger
Trix Wetter

Jacqueline Burckhardt is an art historian and Co-publisher and Senior Editor of *Parkett* magazine, Zurich/New York.

Bice Curiger is Editor in Chief of *Parkett* and Curator at the Kunsthaus, Zurich. She is author of the monograph, *Meret Oppenheim: Defiance in the Face of Freedom,* published in German in 1982 and in English in 1989.

Josef Helfenstein is Curator of the Prints and Drawings Department and of the Paul Klee Foundation at the Kunstmuseum Bern. His writings on Meret Oppenheim, Paul Klee, Louise Bourgeois, and other artists have been published widely.

Thomas McEvilley has written numerous books, catalogue essays, and articles on contemporary art and culture, many of which have been translated into sixteen languages. He teaches art history at Rice University and is a contributing editor to *Artforum*.

Nancy Spector is Associate Curator at the Solomon R. Guggenheim Museum in New York. She has published frequently on contemporary art, including works on Rebecca Horn, Felix Gonzalez-Torres, and Luc Tuymans.

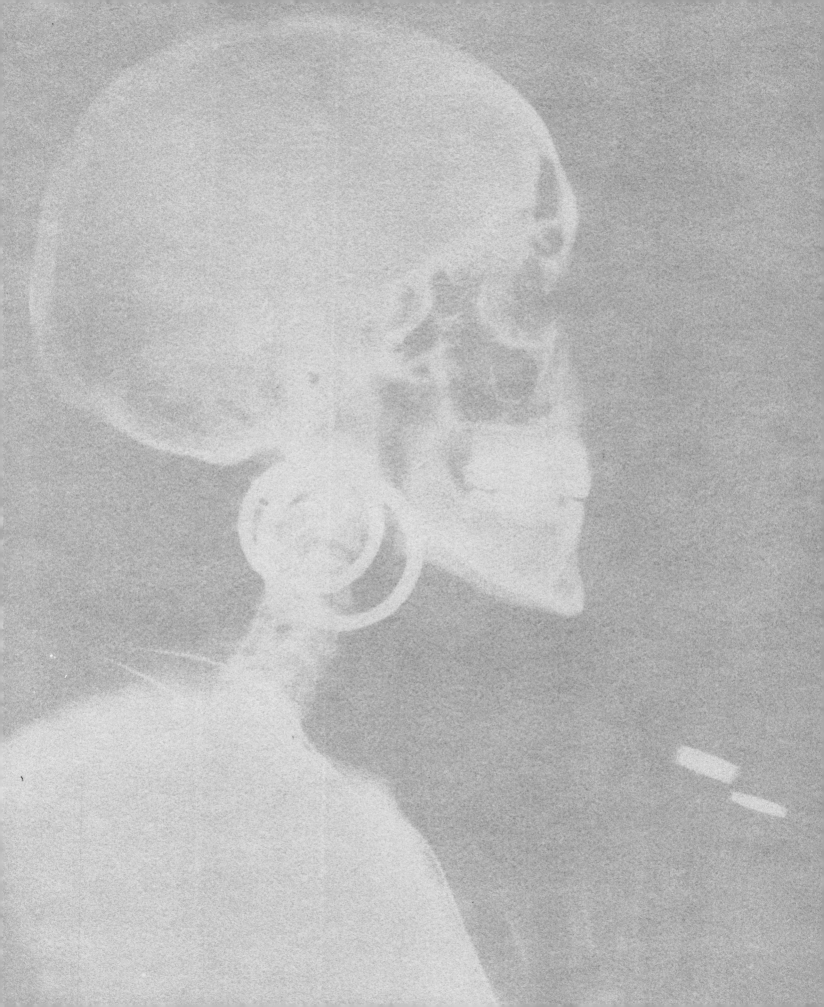

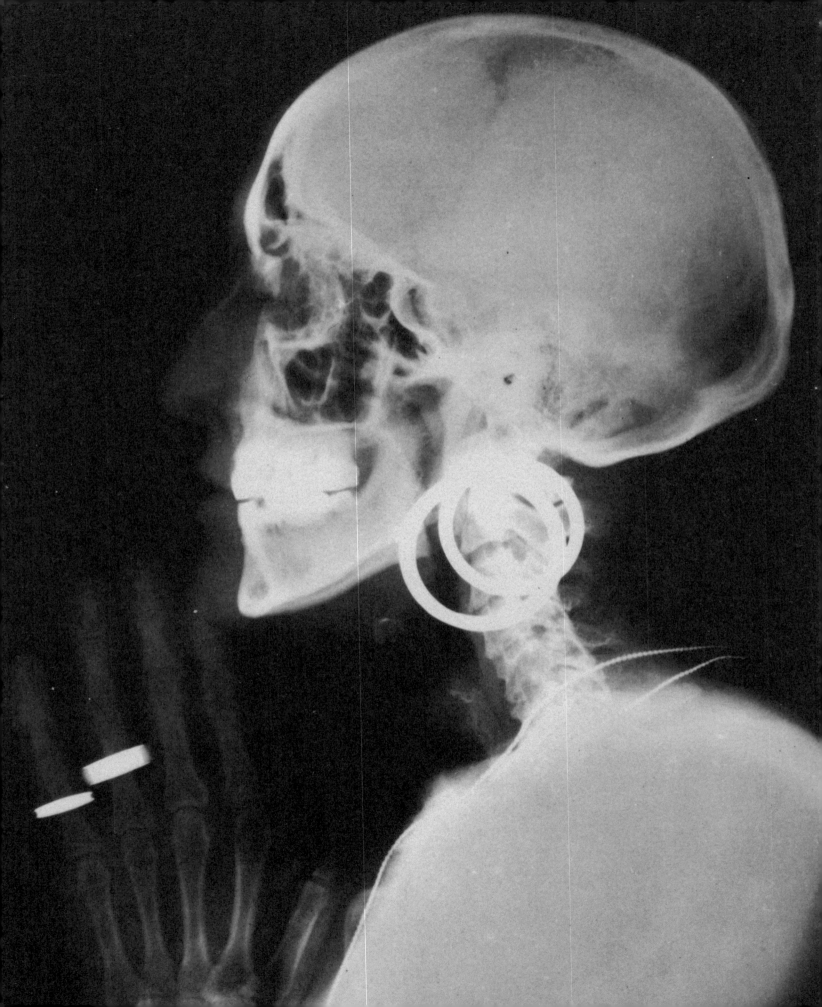